Dedication

This book is dedicated to all those who fought for our freedom and to those who kept the home fires burning here in Clallam County, Washington, *HERE ON THE HOME FRONT*.

Clallam County Memorial in Port Angeles, at the Veterans Memorial park next to the Clallam County Courthouse. Photo by Lonnie Archibald.

Here On the Home Front

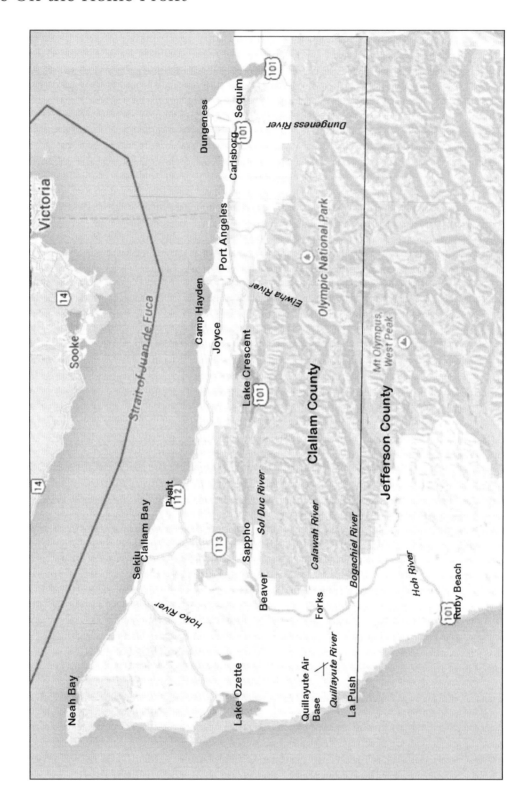

WWII in Clallam County

Facing page: Map of Clallam County, Washington with locations referenced in this book.

Here On the Home Front

HERE ON THE HOME FRONT

WWII IN CLALLAM COUNTY

By

Lonnie Archibald

Lonnie Archibald

Here On the Home Front

Copyright 2014 by Lonnie Archibald

All Rights Reserved

Published by Olympus Multimedia, Forks, Washington

Printed by CreateSpace, an Amazon.com Company

Title ID: 5149976

ISBN-13: 978-1505371161

Acknowledgements

Most of the information obtained for this book was gathered from interviews conducted by the author with those Clallam County residents who remembered the events that took place during World War II here on the home front in Clallam County, Washington.

Thanks to Larry Burtness for his editing abilities and his access to several of the photos used in this book. Also thanks to the Forks Timber Museum, Bert Fletcher, the late Harvey Green, Ron Shearer, Doug McInnes and the *Ditchwalker*, Adria Fuhrman, Greg Munson, Bob and Judy Stipe, and a special thanks to all those who took the time to share their memories of the WW II years.

Table of Contents

Introduction 1
Here on the Home Front.. 3
Where Were You on December 7, 1941?..................................... 5
Soldiers and Camps 13
Railway Cannon 43
USCG Station Ediz Hook 45
Fairchild Airport 47
Camp Hayden.. 49
Lake Ozette and Beach Patrols 55
La Push Beach Patrol Station 65
Naval Auxiliary Air Station, Quillayute 67
The Commissioning Ceremony 73
Remembering Quillayute... 77
Power Plants... 85
Quillayute School Fire... 95
Blimp Crash at Quillayute 97
Quillayute Quill 103
Tuffy and Taffy 105
Liberty Bus 107
Rocket Range.. 109
Housing 113
Japanese Paper Balloon Bombs.. 117
Blackouts 121
Rations 129
Airplane Spotters.. 147
War Bonds.. 157
V-Mail... 163
USO Club 167
Victory Gardens.. 169
Farming, Gardening & Canning.. 173
Industry.. 183
Logging Spruce 189

Here On the Home Front

Women in the Work Place 193
Social Life 199
Wings Cigarettes 217
Scrap Metal Drives and Recyclables 219
Steel War Pennies 223
Tax Tokens 225
War Time News 227
Wreckage of the Lamut 231
Lamut Tea Cup 235
Other Stories and Such 237
Rumors and the Like 249
Rumors Not Substantiated 253
A Letter from Pa 255
VE and VJ Day "The War is Over" 259
Historic Background 265
Post War 267
Blue and Gold Stars 269
Memorials 271
Index 277

Introduction

Within the pages of this book I wish to share with you some of those stories told during interviews with those who experienced those days of WWII here in Clallam County, Washington. Oh, I suppose their stories will differ, as not all saw each event the same. Dates may also vary somewhat as will names and places, but then this is not intended to be a history lesson, you see. Just a few stories told by those who reminisced on the way it was back in the early 1940's. I will assure you this, however, after you have read through these pages and viewed the photos you will have a better understanding of the way it was during WWII here in Clallam County. *Here on the Home Front.*

Lonnie Archibald, Author

Here On the Home Front

On This Day In History...

Thursday, December 03, 1942

Top News Headlines This Week:

Dec 3 - E Delporte discovers asteroid #1560 Strattonia   Dec 4 - 1st US citizenship granted an alien on foreign soil (James Hoey)   Dec 4 - FDR orders dismantling of Works Progress Administration   Dec 4 - US bombers struck Italian mainland for 1st time in WWII   Dec 4 - Works Progress Administration liquidated   Dec 4 - Y Vaisala discovers asteroid #1883 Rimito

Top Songs for 1942

Jersey Bounce by Benny Goodman   *Moonlight Cocktail* by Glenn Miller
Tangerine by Jimmy Dorsey   *Blues In the Night* by Woody Herman
Kalamazoo by Glenn Miller   *White Christmas* by Bing Crosby
He Wears a Pair of Silver Wings by Kay Kyser   *Jingle, Jangle, Jingle* by Kay Kyser
Sleepy Lagoon by Harry James   *Somebody Else Is Taking My Place* by Benny Goodman

1942 Prices
- **Bread:** $0.09/loaf
- **Milk:** $0.60/gal
- **Eggs:** $0.61/doz
- **Car:** $1,100
- **Gas:** $0.20/gal
- **House:** $7,573
- **Stamp:** $0.03/ea
- **Avg Income:** $2,348/yr
- **Min Wage:** $0.30/hr
- **DOW Avg:** 119

US President
Franklin D. Roosevelt

US Vice President
Henry A. Wallace

Academy Award Winners
- **Best Picture:** *Mrs. Miniver* Directed By William Wyler
- **Best Actor:** James Cagney in *Yankee Doodle Dandy*
- **Best Actress:** Greer Garson in *Mrs. Miniver*

People born on December 3
- 1927 - Ferlin Husky country singer (Born to Lose, Gone)
- 1948 - Ozzy Osbourne England, rock vocalist (Black Sabbath-Bark at the Moon)
- 1943 - Valerie Perrine Galveston TX, actress (Slaughterhouse 5)
- 1930 - Andy Williams, Wall Lake Iowa, singer (Moon River, Andy Williams Show)
- 1923 - Maria Callas opera singer

Top Books in 1942

The Matchlock Gun by Walter D. Edmonds   *Black Lamb and Grey Falcon* by Rebecca West
West with the Night by Beryl Markham

A fact list from the war years, December 3, 1942.

Here on the Home Front

Clallam County during World War II

By Lonnie Archibald.

It was Sunday December 7, 1941 and I suppose like many Sundays across this nation families were attending churches, social gatherings, picnics or perhaps splitting fire wood for that old cook stove that stood there in the kitchen. Tommy Dorsey's music was perhaps playing on the radio and in the Sequim Dungeness Valley cattle fed on shucks of hay in the field while in the West End timber awaited the Monday morning logger.

In Pearl Harbor, Hawaii, however, at approximately 10:53 a.m. Pacific Standard Time, American troops, ships and planes were under a surprise attack by waves of Japanese bomber and fighter planes. Eight American battleships were either damaged or destroyed as were several destroyers and other floating devices. More than 2,400 Americans were killed with approximately 1,200 wounded.

News of the "sneak attack" was soon broadcast to America via radio bulletins during many popular entertainment programs. America is shocked and many young men volunteer into the U.S. Armed Forces. Although the U.S. was already politically involved in the war it was now time to declare war against its aggressors. On Monday December 8, 1941, U.S. and Britain declared war on Japan and on Thursday December 11, Italy and Germany declared war on the U.S.

Here On the Home Front

My intent is not to cover the war zones of the South Pacific or European theaters but to look at that which took place here in Clallam County, Washington.

To follow the sneak attack on Pearl Harbor were migrations of American soldiers to Clallam and Jefferson counties. Army camps were set up, there were gun installments, beach patrols, black outs, rations, airplane spotters, day to day news casts of war, entertainment, v-mails, steal pennies, women in the work place and more. So let us now look at how our peninsula families were affected during the war years of 1941-1945, *Here on the Home Front.*

Where Were You on December 7, 1941?

Where to start? Oh I suppose one could tell a few stories that were told at a Round Table meeting which was set up in Forks in October of 1999 during the areas Heritage Day's celebration covering the "war years". The talk which was aired over West End radio station KVAC/KLLM by Al Monroe was mc'd by Forks City Attorney/Planner William "Rod" Fleck. Many of the locals who gathered there had their own stories to share. After recording these stories I decided to begin interviewing other Clallam County citizens who also had stories to share. I began with the question "Where Were You on December 7, 1941."

Lawrence Gaydeski of Forks was out of town visiting relatives in Enumclaw, Washington when the news came over the radio that Pearl Harbor had been bombed. His family drove back to Forks immediately. "There was a lot of apprehension and they didn't know exactly what they would be facing." said Lawrence. Gaydeski was in the fifth grade in Forks at the time and remembered Monday morning the 5th and 6th graders getting together in a joined room listening to President Roosevelt's speech for a declaration of war against Japan, calling the previous day "A Date Which Will Live in Infamy." "There was anger and a certain amount of fear," said Lawrence. It was believed at the time that the Japanese, if they landed, would do so at Kalaloch as well as other Pacific Ocean beaches. "There were plans being made for people to be evacuated in the event of something like that happening," said Lawrence.

Wally Crippen of Forks was up in the hills stringing telephone

Here On the Home Front

wires for air raid stations and heard it on the radio he was carrying. Crippen later joined the Army and in 2004 received the Jubilee of Liberty medal from France for his part in the 1944 invasion at Normandy.

Virginia Blomgren also of Forks, was at Fort Lewis near Tacoma when the war broke out and all pandemonium broke loose. Her folks had come from Forks to pick up family and dropped Virginia (who was attending business college at the time) off at the fort to visit her then boyfriend and future husband Joe Blomgren. While they were there they heard the live account of the bombing on a radio in a car next to them while Joe was changing a tire. Virginia's folks thinking nothing would happen yet, left her and drove to Tacoma. Then all at once loads of soldiers came screaming through the gate and all kinds of military equipment was going out and it was announced over a loud speaker that all visitors had to leave the base. A kind officer gave Joe, who was a new recruit, permission to stand with Virginia outside the gate to wait for her folks to return from Tacoma.

She got to see everything. "It was pure pandemonium," said Virginia. She was about to finish business college and wanted to stay. That night a Seattle radio station announced that it was interment that Seattle would be bombed. Virginia stayed in a boarding house on first hill to finish school, returning to Forks after graduation at the end of December.

John Leppell of Forks was eleven years old when the bombing happened. As an eleven year old boy hearing of the bombing on the radio and seeing soldiers in uniform for the first time was really thrilling to him. As he remembered they arrived in Forks within a very few hours and stayed in the American Legion Hall which at that time was located at 221 N Forks Ave across from where Sully's Drive-In is located today.

Jim Crippen of Forks was boarding with his sister on the Bogachiel while working for Brager Brothers Logging. They got up early Monday morning and heard the news on the radio while they were getting ready to go to work. That was the first they had heard of the bombing. The next month Jim left for Port Angeles to report for duty in the service then off to Fort Lewis. Jim and his Forks buddies Art Anderson, Duncan Smith, Ray Burr, and Ed Maneval of Clallam Bay needed a ride to Port Angeles and since they were all good customers of the old Arts Place Tavern in Forks, owner Art Arnold took them to Port Angeles in a 1937 Chevy but before leaving Forks Arnold filled the trunk with beer. "We stopped at Lake Crescent for a picnic while on our way to Port Angeles and had a pretty good time. I couldn't tell you much more about what happened in Forks during the war 'cause I was gone for a few years," said Jim.

Ted Spoelstra of Forks was living in Seattle at the time attending the University of Washington and living in a boarding house with about thirty other fellows and you can about imagine the intensity of feelings that morning when the announcement was made of the bombing. "Fellows our age under these circumstances knew that our lifestyle was going to be changed one way or another without any question," remarked Ted. It just happened to be the end of the fall quarter at the UW so very few

Here On the Home Front

of that group even bothered to register for the next quarter. We just took off and started doing what we knew we would have to do, seeing the recruiting officers and various other things. So of these thirty fellows, I have seen very few since, and that is quite a loss," said Ted.

My Uncle Larry McHone of Sequim wrote me of his recollection of Pearl Harbor and it went like this.

> On December 7th, 1941 myself and a group of my Carlsborg friends decided to go up on the hill on the south side of Atterberry Road. My brother Frank McHone (better known as Pete) and some other teenagers were on the hill cutting wood. I had just reached the age of 10 and my brother was 17. I don't remember all of them that day but most of the time it was a group of the Dunlap family, Fred Cramer, the Jansen boys, the Hookers, and the Banksons'. After we arrived on the hill another group of teenagers came up from Carlsborg and broke the news to us about the attack on Pearl Harbor. All the information came over the radio and that shocked everyone in our group and we were mad as hell that the Japanese had bombed us although most of us didn't know where Pearl Harbor was located. Radio was our only contact with the rest of the world since TV did not exist in our area at that time.
>
> Our troops from Fort Lewis and Fort Worden started preparing for an attack on our Olympic Peninsula. Soldiers started coming into Sequim, Carlsborg, Dungeness and Agnew to set up defensive positions along the straits. Living just south of the Carlsborg School, I remember watching Army trucks and jeeps driving by our home. The soldiers were friendly and the locals helped them when needed. I remember the women, including my mother Eva McHone, offering to do their laundry for a small fee just to cover the cost of the soap.
>
> Every day for some time our roads were busy with army equipment and soldiers. The soldiers really liked to get acquainted with the young lady's in the area. Our sky became busy with airplanes, one group came from the Port Angeles Airport. One airplane lost its power and the pilot bailed out and survived but the plane crashed in some trees somewhere south of highway 101. They would fly low between the highway and school.

John and June Nelson of Port Angeles told of their experience of December 7, 1941. "We were at a friend's house in Seattle when the phone rang and the friend's husband answered saying "Yes Sir, Yes Sir, I'll be right there," slammed the receiver down and ran into the bedroom. As Nelson's friend was wondering what was going on, the young soldier came back out in his military uniform. He had just been told of the bombing of Pearl Harbor. He had to go immediately. They then turned the radio on and heard President Roosevelt make the announcement of the bombing." said June.

John and June remembered driving back to Port Angeles that afternoon and were stopped by soldiers at Discovery Bay. "They already had a convoy there with guns and everything. We were sandwiched into the convoy of Army vehicles and had to stay with them all the way to Port Angeles," remarked John. "The soldiers said if we tried to leave the convoy we would be shot at," said June. They also asked why the Nelsons were there and why they were going to Port Angeles.

Marge Deinis of Port Angeles was in church when she heard of the bombing. "There were several young men in the congregation and they were very upset not knowing where they would be the next day. Some were drafted right away and some joined the Navy." said Marge.

Betty (Ryser) Dunlap remembered she was at the Sequim high School Auditorium trying out for the Senior Play when it was announced on the radio of the bombing of Pearl Harbor. She also mentioned that the next day there was an assembly at school

Here On the Home Front

where they heard President Franklin Roosevelt's speech declaring war on Japan.

My mother, Vay (McHone) Dunlap-Archibald, remembered, while living at Washington Harbor near Sequim, had made the trip with my dad Delbert (Nig) Dunlap down towards Dungeness to get apples from one of the Cameron Farms and heard the news there. "Many were in disbelief. They couldn't believe it could happen to the United States." One of my longtime friends, Henry Echternkamp was killed at Pearl Harbor when the battleship Arizona was attacked by the Japanese. The VFW post in Sequim was named after him," said mother. Another of mothers friends killed during the war was Marlyn Nelson. His memorial now stands at Port Williams.

Ron Shearer of Forks was 13 and living at the north end of what today is Spartan Ave at the junction with Calawah Way next to where the telephone central office now sits. "Right behind us was a group of cabins they called Spooners Park and I remember Gene Foster's folks lived in one of the bigger cabins. Somehow or other I happened to go over there in the morning and they were all clustered around the radio and I heard what was happening and I ran back over to our house yelling, "turn on the radio, things are blowing up, the Japanese have bombed Pearl Harbor. And that's how we heard of the bombing," said Ron.

Bob Bowlby of Clallam Bay was a high school student when the bombing took place and was visiting his grandpa William Morton Bowlby in Forks that Sunday morning when it came over the radio that the Japanese had bombed Pearl Harbor. Almost immediately the army came to Clallam Bay with the first jeeps we ever saw and they were towing 37mm gun mounts. "They towed them around a while before they got any shells," remarked Bob.

John Jarvis of Agnew was at the Elwha Theater in Port Angeles taking in an afternoon matinee when the projector was shut off and it was announced that Pearl Harbor had been bombed. "We went straight home," said John.

Bert Fletcher of Port Angeles was in the first grade in Forks when Pearl Harbor was bombed. "We were all talking about it the following Monday morning and a lot of the kids were saying "did you hear they even bombed Seattle?" And there were all kinds of rumors going around and of course we had already heard about war because you heard on the radio all the time about occupied France and the Germans fighting in Africa and so on. A lot of us didn't really understand what it was all about but we eventually learned from our teachers what it was," said Bert.

"I remember the day the war started. My mother and step father were cutting fire wood and my older sister Jean and I were outside and she had the radio on when they announced that the Japanese had just bombed Pearl Harbor. My sister panicked and said 'My God we are at war,' and I said Oh, ok, then she explained to me what war was. I was six years old and attending Beaver School at the time," said Pat (Blevins) Mansfield of Forks.

Here On the Home Front

Soldiers and Camps

Ron Shearer of Forks remembered the first military that came to Forks was the Washington State Guard. "It seemed like they were just young kids. I mean 15 & 16 years old. They were like a Boy Scout Troop. I wasn't much younger but I remember looking at those guys and thinking boy if they are our front line we are in trouble," said Ron. But they were only here for a short time then the US Army came in. Ron remembered an Army camp set up near where Sully's Drive-In is today and also at Quillayute, the Bogachiel bridge south of Forks, and another at Ruby Beach. There was a big military presence. "We had no idea of the power Japan had, none whatsoever," remarked Ron.

The first thing the military did was to set up road blocks at all the river bridges. You would stop at the Calawah Bridge and give them your ID papers and so forth. At night someone would shine a flashlight on you and you would show your ID. Up on the bank above the road would be a sandbag emplacement and you would be looking up the barrel of a machine gun. Every one of the bridges had someone there twenty four hours a day.

June Nelson shared this story about bridge checks. "There were four of us women and one had a cabin out at "The Place" near Joyce and we had been out there for the weekend and when we came home Sunday afternoon in our personal vehicle across the Elwha Bridge we recognized the soldier at the bridge who had checked us on our way out Friday. Just for fun, when stopped and asked if we were all that were in the vehicle, I said "We got a little Jap in the trunk" and they made us all get out and we thought it was so funny until we all got bald out." Well that was the last time the girls pulled that little trick. They had learned to answer correctly. There were check points at all river bridges as it was thought if there was a Japanese infiltration we would blow up the bridges," said John Nelson. Bob Bowlby of Clallam Bay was sure the bridges were wired with explosives.

Boyd Rupp, who worked out of Hoquiam and other areas in the mid-1930's as a Washington State Patrolman, was transferred to Forks in early 1942 as the US Government figured the Japanese were going to invade the northwest and particularly the Olympic Peninsula. Boyd soon found himself dressed in tin pants, a tin hat and caulk boots. "I lived in them for six months," said Boyd. He patrolled the beaches carrying a 30/30 rifle that the State Game Department had confiscated from poachers.

Boyd was to get the word out if anything of a suspicious nature showed up. He had to routinely check all the old cabins and homesteads along the Pacific Beaches here in the West End. The government figured the Japanese would first send a scouting party. His job was to watch for any signs of these invaders. He wore logging clothing and carried no identification for six months before the government knew for sure where all the Japanese fleet was located.

He also told of a military police underground headquarters at Ruby Beach, located south of Forks and north of Kalaloch. Boyd had to deliver messages to the police by way of a vehicle with blacked-out headlights. The police would holler "Halt," then check you over while holding machine guns on you. Later the government organized a coast guard beach patrol that used attack dogs. "Those were wicked dogs," said Boyd. There were 28 dogs kept at La Push in cages. "They would eat you for lunch if they had the chance," remarked Boyd.

According to historical data compiled by the Coast Guard, the La Push Coast Guard Station was a Beach Patrol Station established In September of 1942 and discontinued March 29, 1944. The Beach Patrols at Ozette patrolled from Point of Arches to the north side of Cape Johnson and the Coast Guard Lifeboat Station at La Push patrolled north to Cape Johnson and south to Goodman Creek. It has been said that the wartime logbooks of beach patrol stations were destroyed by the Coast Guard after the war. Walkie-Talkie's weighing about 12 pounds each with a range of about 5 miles were being tested by the Beach Patrol stations along the north Washington coast at both La Push and Ozette in January of 1943. If they proved this equipment valuable they would be ordered for all stations. No cell phones back then you see. By February of 1943 the La Push Beach Patrol Station was in full operation. A continuous patrol was also being maintained at Port Angeles by January, 1943.

Truck transportation was established wherever possible to and from patrol stations. Some horse patrols were established where there were stretches of sandy beaches. In the wilderness territory, however, patrols were to proceed by trails to the beach front. The patrolmen were to carry firearms, bedding, including sleeping bags, protective clothing and food for their 24 hour tours of duty. By February 1943 approximately 640 officers and

Here On the Home Front

men were assigned to the entire Washington beaches.

By March 15, 1944 Beach Patrol activity at Baada Point Life Boat station at Neah Bay was discontinued and effective April 1, 1944, Baada Point Life Boat Station was placed in an inactive status. Lifeboat station duties were then performed by personnel at the Coast Guard Base. Also by the end of March 1944 patrols at La Push, Ozette and Kalaloch (in Jefferson County) were discontinued.

The Army Camp on the Bogachiel River south of Forks.
Dorothy Burr Collection.

Lawrence Gaydeski of Forks remembered troops coming to the Kalaloch/Ruby Beach area within a few days of the Pearl Harbor bombing. Lawrence told a story of his dad Steven Gaydeski who at that time was running road grader for the State Highway out of Forks. The road south to Kalaloch was gravel during the war years you see and so Steven would make one or two trips a week south of town to grade the crude but passable roadway. On one particular day Steven, well we will just call him Steve, was grading road during a rainy day near Ruby Beach when he was flagged down by a man alongside the road. Well the man turned out to be a US soldier asking Steve where he got the rain coat. "In Forks," replied Steve. "Where is Forks?" asked the soaked soldier. "About twenty five miles north of here," replied Lawrence's dad. "Can you get me one?" asked the soldier. Yes said Steve and that he did, delivering the rain gear on the next trip down. Well it turned out that the man was a GI who with his company was dropped off there in the wilderness of swamp water and salmon berry bushes poorly prepared without even any rain clothing. According to Steve, they were camped there for nearly a month before they even had a kitchen, just living on K-rations. On the following trip to the ocean he found more soldiers asking for rain gear. They gave Steve the money and he obliged by purchasing the much sought-for clothing from a business in Forks ran by a Mr. Steve Clark. By this time Steve Gaydeski had purchased about all the available rain gear in Forks. Well, finally Mr. Clark asked Steve what he was doing with all the clothing and Steve told him he was buying it for the guys on the state highway crew. At that time the Army didn't want the world to know where they were located. But then I have my doubts if the world knew where Kalaloch and Ruby Beach

Here On the Home Front

were anyway.

It was somewhat later that Marge Deinis and June Nelson of Port Angeles, who volunteered with the United Service Organization (USO) Red Cross located in the basement of the Elks building, would make the trip from Port Angeles to Ruby Beach. They would visit all the military Camps while traveling in the back of a truck which had only one small back window. Ruby Beach Camp was one of those where the ladies would deliver coffee and donuts to the young men who would protect us from a Japanese beach invasion should it occur.

George Wood of Port Angeles, who was working at Crown Zellerbach mill during the war, told of soldiers bivouacked in garages or wherever they could find an area up on the hill where he lived on West 6th Street. Actually they were camped all over Lincoln Heights according to George. They had machine guns along 4th, 5th, and 6th Streets there on the bluff overlooking the Strait and downtown Port Angeles. "The place was fortified," said George. George also remembered cutting 4X4 paper blankets at the mill for those poor soldiers. "The soldiers didn't have a thing when they came here, not even cartridges for their guns until a week after they arrived. There was also a machine gun nest there on top of the Crown Zellerbach mill," said George. George also mentioned that the Navy had moved in to the Coast Guard Station on Ediz Hook. They even had their own football and baseball teams. Soldiers also set up camp at Crown Zellerbach in a room about 14X20 where the mill would hold their meetings. That was turned over to the Army along with a few of the mill sheds.

On Quillayute Prairie, west of Forks, Ed Duncan remembered Army soldiers in 1939 living in the old Quillayute Store then in Quonset huts built just north-east of the airport. Ed remembered at that time there was the cemetery, a store, restaurant, hotel, cabins, church and school. The school burned down in December, 1941. At that time there was only one graveled runway at The Quillayute Airport. In 1942 and 43 soldiers also camped in tents near the church.

Sequim school student Doug McInnes remembered the Sequim High School holding an assembly for students who left early for the service. This was in March and April of 1942. They did graduate however.

In Port Angeles; John Nelson remembered soldiers staying in the Masonic Temple as well as a lot of other large buildings around town. Soldiers also stayed at the old Moose Hall, a stone structure located along Lincoln Street.

Betty (Ryser) Dunlap, Toni (Becker) Kettle and June (Ryser) Matriotti remembered soldiers stationed in the Sequim High School Gym, the Seals mercantile building down town, the WRC (Women's Relief Corp) where the VFW sits today, Dungeness School, and the Agnew Community Hall, Betty remembered having lunch with the soldiers at the Sequim school lunchroom. The ladies also remembered ridding and also driving out across Matriotti's fields in the Army jeeps with the soldiers. And what a sight it must have been with birds scurrying about and girls laughing as the brown colored jeeps made way across the cow pastures and Alfalfa fields there in the Sequim-Dungeness

Here On the Home Front

Valley. June also spoke of the time while living on her parents farm on the east end of town that a soldier was cleaning his gun, it went off and the bullet whizzed by her head. "That was scary," said June.

Also in the August 2001 issue of "The Ditchwalker" published for Sequim Old-Timers and given to me by Doug McInnes of Jamestown I found this article written by Lewis Dey, Sequim High School class of 1948, and it went like this:

IT WAS A GREAT RIDE!

During WWII 'School children were encouraged to purchase war stamps and bonds in their classrooms. With a bond purchase we were given a thrilling ride in an Army Jeep. As sixth grade students we filled the Jeep to capacity and were driven out through the old growth trees surrounding the baseball field. The Jeep careened through the timber while we yelled with joy-and sometimes screamed in terror -hanging on for dear life while the 18 year old G.I. driver enjoyed his assigned duty.

Sixty years later I still remember the thrill of that ride! How would our safety-conscious society of today accept this type of reward for supporting the war effort? School administrators would be quick to say "NO." things haven't always changed for the better. Lewis Dey, class of '48.

Out West in Neah Bay, Darrel (Bub) Elvrum had moved from Clallam Bay to Neah Bay in 1940 when his folks moved there with the intentions of starting a restaurant. They rented a two story house and made the bottom part a restaurant. It was called "The Bay View". Later they moved to a new location and built Elvrum's Resort where they built cabins and a trailer park. They rented out to mostly fisherman. The crew that built the breakwater in the Makah Harbor was by that time leaving town.

The construction crew was finishing up the breakwater which stretched out to Waadah Island from the mainland. This structure built of large rock was built to protect the harbor so boats which were to protect the coast could anchor up. There were patrol boats such as the "Black Douglas".

"I had an uncle who was in the Navy aboard that boat," said Bub. The boats would come in for provisions and some would stay a while before moving out to patrol the coast. There was a dock just east of where the USCG Base is today. "There were pretty good sized Navy ships that came in," said Bub. According to Bub there were probably 45 to 50 some Navy personnel there at the base which was just east of the present USCG Base. Bub remembered the barracks and a gym which after the war became the Crown Zellerbach building then the Makah Tribal office. The Job Corp had also used the barracks. The Army also had a camp out at Sooes west of Neah Bay during the war. They were typical wooden buildings with tar paper.

"I remember when we were in the restaurant in the early 40's just after the war started our dishes started rattling and we couldn't figure out what that was from. We went outside, looked up the graveled road and here came some Army tanks around the comer. Then came a mule train for packing to the outposts. They had a bunch of mules to pack supplies to Shi-Shi and the coastal beaches," said Bub. They finally completed a road out to Shi Shi Beach. Bub also remembered the old portable radar which was located out on a rock bluff along the Sooes River. Permanent Radar was later installed at Bahokus Peak just east of the old Air Force Base (which is now the Makah Tribal Office) and north of the Waatch River. Bub also remembered a pillbox with a 20mm gun on Anderson Point south-west of the mouth of the Sooes River. There were also two 29 mm guns with an ammunition bunker located on a 100 foot high cliff between the old Air Force Base and Cape Flattery.

You could see all the beach from Waatch to Anderson Point. There was a bus that traveled back and forth between Neah Bay and Port Angeles. It was often faster, however, for the servicemen to hitchhike as civilians would pick them up. You would never see a servicemen standing alongside the road very long, even if it were only a couple miles up the road to their destination, someone would pick them up. "We got to know them pretty well," said Bub. There was also an Army Camp set up just east of the existing cemetery on the water side of the flat along Neah Bay Road. It was a large tent with ship lap flooring. There was also a pill box and gun set up where you could see east all the way up to Sail River.

Bub remembered construction crews driving pilling for a railroad from the mainline to Waadah Island. The rocks for the jetty were then hauled out there by train. The rails ran all the way out to the rock quarry just east of where the tribal office is today along the Waatch River where the Air Force Base once stood. They drilled and blasted an 8x8 coyote hole back in the mountain of rock. They would go back in there and make a "T" then they would bring in truckloads of powder canisters, load them on a little rail cart, push them back in there and touch them off. "I figured when they started blasting, about half the buildings in Neah Bay would fall down. You didn't hear any bang, it was just a tremble and you wouldn't see rock flying any place, just staying right there. They had some good powder monkeys," remarked Bub. They would load the rocks on railroad dump cars and carry them out to the jetty site. They worked around the clock. Another army outpost Bub remembered was farther east on the strait at Shipwreck Point. They had tents back in and away from the beach. Also there used to be an old car body sitting up on the bank along Highway 112 at Freshwater Bay near where the Holly farm sits. Two guards with rifles would stop you, check your ID, and look your car over. Bub also spoke of guard dogs which were kept in kennels at the Navy Base and also at the USCG. There were also Army tanks dug into the sand at Hobuck Beach where they could watch Makah Bay.

John Leppell also mentioned the Army Camp at Ruby Beach which was located across the road from where the Ruby Beach store sat. According to John and Elizabeth (Huelsdonk) Fletcher they had built their first beach cabin there in 1928. This was to become a resort with fifteen cabins and a store with living quarters and a gas pump. The store operated until late 1941 or early 1942 when the U.S. Army took over. The store was opened once again after the war. Those who then leased the resort from the ONP were the Secrists, Walkers, Gronseths and Fullertons, but not necessarily in that order. The Olympic National Park tore the resort down in 1960.

John Leppell still has the old maple butcher block out of the Ruby Beach Amy camp. He used it at his Forks butcher shop for several years. John had purchased it from a person who bought it from the Army after the war. John heard that there were eventually 300 soldiers at the Ruby Beach camp. They eventually had power plants, a kitchen, a bakery, a mechanic shop and more.

Inez Halverson of Forks, (we just called her Halvi), remembered soldiers staying in tents on the Bogachiel River south of Forks on the south side of the river across from where the Bogachiel State Park is today. She thought the Signal Corp was staying there while installing telephone lines for the Coast Guard. "They were there for about six months then another group came in after the first had left. One of the groups consisted of black soldiers," said Halvi. Halvi also remembered while living nearby, her family and several neighbors inviting these soldiers to their homes for holidays such as Thanksgiving and Christmas. One soldier with the last name of Dominique sent her v-mail from Italy after being shipped overseas. He also sent Halvi Christmas cards up until the early 2000's. There were other soldiers who would also send her cards. Halvi also remembered men from Huelsdonk and Smith Mills working to build the kitchen at the Quillayute Air Base west of Forks.

Dorothy (Smith) Burr whose parents had the Bogachiel store also remembered the camp and thought the Black soldiers were there in the spring of 1942 then white soldiers came later. Smith kept his store open for longer hours while the camp was there.

Ron Shearer also remembered the camp on the Bogachiel. The reason they were down there was to cut telephone poles," said Ron. Down south of the Bogachiel River just north of the

Huling's mill was a patch of cedar trees the group would cut for poles. "Someone had filled these guys with so much BS about bears that they were scared to death they would run into one of those dreaded creatures and so they had to have a guy with a gun standing on a stump wherever they went. They wouldn't get off the graveled road without an armed guard. These were a good bunch of guys and we would all go swimming down there just above the Bogachiel Bridge. They were good to us kids," said Ron. According to Ron the coast guard had a phone line all the way from Neah Bay to San Francisco. When I went to work for Peninsula Telephone and Telegraph company in 1969 there was still coast guard open wire in the Forks area.

Ron who lived next to the old telephone office in Forks during the war remembered Boyd Schlacter being a one man telephone company. There were Coast Guard guys who numbered about a dozen that would show up for work there as they stayed with Forks families around town paying for roam and board. "These guys would show up every morning with their trucks ready to go to work and since this was Schlaeter's area for telephones he was the boss. Of course Schlaeter would coordinate with the person who was in charge of the Coast Guard crew," said Ron.

Ron, like a few others, also mentioned the Army camp at Ruby Beach located on the east side of the highway across from where the road to the Ruby Beach parking lot is today. "I remember going back in there after the war and it was all painted camouflaged colors with the roof lines, kind of swirl like, and you had to get within fifty feet of the camp or you couldn't see it. "The military stationed there would patrol the beaches," said Ron.

Here On the Home Front

In later years, Warren Paul of Forks remembered that on his first hike from Sand Point Beach to Rialto he seen some kind of a lookout tower clear up on top of a sandy knoll near the Norwegian Memorial. There were broken down ladders and such but it was all gone the last time he was there. Warren was sure it had been used by the USCG or Beach Patrol during the war.

Myron Simmons spoke of the USCG base at La Push when during the war the base stood on the hill where the school is today. There was a large water tank and a lookout tower where the military would watch out over the Pacific with binoculars in search of enemy planes. There was also a lifeboat station just below the Coast Guard building on the Quillayute River where the Rivers Edge Restaurant is today.

My mother Vay (McHone) Dunlap-Archibald remembered while living in Carlsborg during the war seeing soldiers staying in the old show house. "I was working at the Carlsborg store and I had to walk right past them every day and the soldiers would be upstairs in that old show building. They would be looking down and that would make me nervous so I would walk on the other side of the street to get to the store. They were all real nice however. My mother Eva (Bodenhaufer) McHone-Taylor invited soldiers in once in a while to have a meal especially on holidays and they were always real nice people," said mother.

Marge (McDonald) Cowan-Jenson of Beaver remembered Soldiers camping in tents near the John Cowan Place in a field along where the Little Hoko River runs into the Hoko. Marge also mentioned that the USCG had barracks at Lake Ozette and the

USCG at Neah Bay having 12 police dogs which would patrol from Neah Bay to Ozette. "They walked the beaches in shifts," said Marge.

Betty (Pedersen) Bernier of Forks remembered while living at Tyee, known today as Beaver, there were soldiers living in Joe Sylvia's cabins behind the store. "There were about 22 or so cabins and when the war broke out a lot of army soldiers and their families were living there in those cabins," said Betty. "I remember this one old gal had this great big black car, like a hearse, and she would go up and down the streets of Tyee and she would say "Run for the hills, Run for the hills."

Here On the Home Front

A U.S. Army encampment on the John Cowan farm on the Hoko River. The farm is now owned by the Washington State Parks. Friends of Clallam Bay Library Photo Collection.

Ron Shearer mentioned little spots where the Coast Guard and Army would man stations such as the cabins on Hoh Head south of La Push and at Ellen Creek north of Rialto. According to Ron these small cabins were all up and down the coast where the military could watch for suspicious activity.

Ron also mentioned how his mother was always inviting servicemen to their house to hang around and eat with the family. She would mother them as many were lonely. This one soldier from back east named Porky Swank was a regular around the house and was on the Beach Patrol. See Lamut page 235, for his story concerning the wreck of the Lamut.

Glen Price remembered seeing soldiers herding mules down the highway stretching all the way from Beaver to Sappho. "We were going to the Sappho Lookout to watch for airplanes. Don't know where the soldiers were heading," said Glen

Virginia (Huling) Blomgren of Forks also remembered when her mother taught school at the Cassell's on the lower Hoh and also at the Barlow school at Oil City during the war. "There were Coast Guard people stationed down at the mouth of the Hoh River too and they would come up to the lower Hoh (Barlow's) school at the Fred and Lena Fletcher's place at the time and dance as mother had a phonograph in the school. The school room would still be warm from the old wood stove and we would dance and visit, then they would walk back down river to their camp," said Virginia. Virginia and her husband Joe reminisced of war time songs such as *Rum and Coca Cola*, *Don't Fence Me In* and The White Cliffs of Dover. "It was an interesting era and of course everybody worried about the war because it was pretty scary there for a while," said Virginia.

Joe remembered the Army Signal Corps building the telephone lines from Neah Bay to Hoquiam during the war. According to Joe the lines were later turned over to the Coast Guard. Joe remembered Elmer Pederson, who later had the Prairie Motel in Forks, working with the Signal Corps at that time. Some of the Signal Corp was camped on the Bogachiel River south of Forks.

U.S. Army Signal Corp recruitment poster. Posters were produced by the War Department to promote a variety of patriotic efforts.

Here On the Home Front

Hoh School at the Barlow's on the lower Hoh River in 1970. The school was built in 1906 and operated as a school until 1943. Photo by Lonnie Archibald.

Walt Fuhrman also remembered the camp on the Bogachiel and claimed that the crew had at first mistakenly cut hemlock rather than cedar poles for the telephone lines. But then one has to wonder if some of those city boys who were from the east coast or the Midwest could really tell a cedar from a fir, a hemlock, or a spruce, they weren't exactly Clallam County lumber jacks you see.

June and Bob Bowlby of Clallam Bay remembered soldiers camping in Green's field which was located about one half mile north of the Pysht junction on the east side of highway 112. Bob also spoke of mule skinners camping along the way as they moved west towards Neah Bay and Ozette. "They would camp every night. They had semi-trucks and would haul mules one day then pack them the next," said Bob. They would trade off hauling and packing the mules as the mules were carrying the components for 75mm Howitzer cannons which were being pulled by the jeeps. So the mules would walk one day then ride the trucks the next.

"I was coming home from Clallam Bay one day on my bicycle and came upon 500 mules," said Bob. He remembered some of the mules pasturing near Sherman Hull's place along Charlie Creek Road which at that time was the old highway. Bob and his wife June also remembered the mules pasturing along the Hoko-Ozette Road a couple miles beyond the Cowan place at the Orsett homestead. "Those mules were no doubt heading for the Lake Ozette area," said Bob. Bob also claimed that most of the soldiers who were packing the mules were southerners who were recruited for their experience handling the beasts.

Here On the Home Front

"I suppose this happened everywhere they stopped but when they were in Clallam Bay they were close enough to have liberty in town and if there was ever a drinking place it was Clallam Bay in the early 40's and with all the loggers here In the country, Clallam Bay was set up to serve a lot of beer," said Bob. "One night a man went out to his truck and got his 30/06 and shot one guy in the neck and I think one man died. I remember my classmate George McGuire was delivering milk as they had a farm outside of town and he got into town when the shooting was going on as he entered with his green 1929 Model "A" with his milk bottles and the like and so he got out of there as soon as he could," said Bob.

The 98th Field Artillery Battalion from Fort Lewis makes its way through Clallam Bay on a training exercise. The 98th Field Artillery was one of five U.S. Army Battalions that used mules to transport artillery where mechanized units could not go. Photo from Friends of Clallam Bay Library Collection.

Bob Bowlby also told of the two cabins at Toleak Point south of La Push that his grandfather built in about 1937. Most of the materials for building were packed in off the beach and he even had his cook stove brought in by a fishing boat. According to Bob, a Charles Edward Cone who was an author and poet from Alaska also stayed in one of the cabins prior to the war. "During the war the Beach Patrol brought in plywood for remodeling to make the rustic cabins more livable. The Beach Patrol also built dog kennels and patrolled the beaches with their dogs," said

Here On the Home Front

Bob. They even had a small generator to run a light plant there along this wilderness beach.

In Sequim Elsie Mae (Gilbert) Manning, class of '43 wrote the following for the November, 2003 issue of The Ditchwalker.

"Remembering Soldiers in the Gym"

On December 7, 1941, my parents and I took a Sunday afternoon drive with the Gaylord Jackson family to the Sol Duc Hot Springs. While listening to the car radio, the announcement was made that Pearl Harbor had been attacked. We immediately returned home and were glued to the radio the rest of the evening, wondering how this would affect us and worrying about my uncle, who was a Navy pilot stationed in San Diego. That night I was awakened by the Army trucks hitting the expansion joints as they crossed the Dungeness Bridge.

Before going to school Monday morning, we learned that an Army unit had moved into the Sequim High School gymnasium during the night. As we headed for school every girl was cautioned not to talk to any of those soldiers and we didn't for a few days. It wasn't long until we learned those soldiers were mostly young men from Seattle with a National Guard medical unit. (Several of my girlfriends later married men from that group.)

The captain of the unit was quartered in the school nurse's office, and after the second week a couple of us approached him about having a dance in the gym for those "poor lonely" soldiers. The soldiers had already been requested to not walk on the gym floor in their boots (had to keep it ready for basketball games), so we suggested a "stocking foot" dance. Permission was given. My dad drove my cousin Sid, Margie Mills and me to the gym. When the dance was over the young ladies were invited to the cafeteria for cocoa and cookies, with the girls escorted to the cafeteria first, and followed by the soldiers. When the time was up, we girls left to be picked up by our parents. While running to the car (with only parking lights showing) the grade school monkey bars caught me on my neck, knocking me out. The cafeteria door opened allowing enough light for all these "medics" to see me in my embarrassment. Needless to say, I was quickly on my feet with mud all over my back.

John Jarvis of Agnew, a small community north west of Carlsborg, remembered a dozen trucks full of soldiers coming to his dad's farm right after the bombing of Pearl Harbor. "There were twenty acres hooked onto this place where I was raised when I was a little kid. They moved in there and set up, what I remember as three of those 155mm Howitzers. They were dug into gun emplacements at the edge of the woods down below ground level with sand bags all around and chicken wire netting on the top with camouflage. All you could see at the end of the field and into the woods were gun barrels. The guns were facing towards the water, Strait of Juan De Fuca, as it was mostly open fields from the woods to the beach at that time," said John. John also remembered the soldiers staying in tents with some staying in their hay barn and also using their Finnish Sauna building to set up their radio equipment and command post. There was also another patch of woods on their property where the soldiers set up a large tent for their kitchen to feed all those hungry soldiers that were camped there. The soldiers, who John believed were with the Army National Guard, left the farm sometime the following spring.

John also remembered in the winter the ground had frozen and was starting to thaw and the soldiers were coming up the driveway with those big six by six GI trucks and they absolutely just tore up the driveway leaving thick mud so bad that John's dad Ero had to park his car out on what now is the Finn Hall Road north of the house. "Dad would then walk to the house as there was no way to get up that driveway since it was tore up so bad," said John.

Here On the Home Front

He also spoke of the steam bath, which was heated by fire wood, being used by the soldiers to keep their bodies warm during those cold winter days and nights. Two to three foot wood chunks would fit fine in the old fifty gallon drum used as a fire box for the Finnish Sauna. Therefore the visiting military personnel were kept busy cutting wood to feed that temporary heater which existed there.

"And then of course when the Army moved out Bob Tulin who was a neighbor of ours, and I would play in those gun emplacements as those were a wonderful place for kids to play. I was ten years old in 1941 so we would play war games and we probably defeated the whole Japanese Army right there," said John.

John remembered the emplacements being all dirt, no cement. The soldiers had dug a long tunnel, well long in John's eyes anyway, about 15 feet back to this room where they kept all their ammunition. It was all covered with timbers and dirt and camouflaged on top with branches and such. The room was away from the guns you see.

"Another thing I remember, in fact there is still one there. Over there where the George Washington Inn stands there were machine gun emplacements looking over the bluff onto the straits. They were just holes dug into the ground with logs in the front of them. One is still there but it's caved in. Just a depression in the ground but you can tell where it was," said John.

Another thing the soldiers left behind was the barbed wire. They had barbed wire entanglements all along everywhere we had a fence. We tried to salvage it later on but it was that real stiff wire and all tangled up and really hard to work with, hard to straighten out but we did use some of it. I remember my grandpa taken and trying to straighten it out and re-using it to make fences after they left. It was there for a long time," said John.

"I do remember when the soldiers left they left us a whole bunch of loaves of bread. Boxes of bread. We ate what we could and fed the rest to the pigs which we were raising at the time," said John. What a sight that must have been with those pigs wallowing in the mud fighting over that last piece of crust here on the farm.

In Sequim, Doug McInnes remembered on March 16, 1942 an Army Lieutenant came to Sequim High School and showed and described a rifle and a 30 caliber machine gun. (Who says no guns in school?)

Doug also wrote the following in the Ditchwalker publication: Things changed fast around Sequim after the war started in 1941. Two Sequim boys at Pearl Harbor were immediate casualties. They were both brothers of two of my sixth grade classmates.

Within days, we had soldiers patrolling the area watching for a Japanese invasion. The soldiers at Jamestown Beach stayed in the Jamestown school. They built machine gun nests along the

Here On the Home Front

beach by day and patrolled the beach by night.

Army men slept in the Sequim school gymnasium for a while. Army medics patched up a couple of my pals who were injured while playing: one hit in the head by a rock and the other run over by a horse while riding his bicycle.

Soldiers helped my family put in hay in the summer of '42. Most were city boys who had never seen a pitchfork. What a mess.

The threat of Japanese attacks was short-lived and most of the soldiers moved on long before the war ended.

Pat (Blevins) Mansfield of Forks living in a cabin on the Rixon Road during the war told of soldiers guarding the two Sol Duc Bridges near Sappho as the bridges were being built on highway 101 but not yet completed. Soldiers who were camped near where Sully's Drive In is today in Forks would come out to Sappho and Pat's sister Jean was fond of one of the young men.

She asked her mother if she could go on patrol with the handsome young soldier but her mother said she would have to take her little sister Pat along on the journey. Well needless to say this really put a damper on her planned adventure. I believe this to be quite common during the war here in Clallam County.

Jim Mansfield also spoke of the Army bringing mules on maneuvers to Forks just prior to the war and camping near the Forks Airport. Due to the fact that the Army brought hay along for the mules Jim blames them for introducing quack grass to the area. "You can't get rid of it," remarked Jim.

Here On the Home Front

Railway Cannon

As told by Steve Hauff

A railroad mounted cannon on a siding in Port Angeles.
Photo from the collection of Steve Hauff.

Very few people knew that the cannons were ever here. They were placed on sidings just west of the end of 6th Street in Port Angeles. They were brought in about February, 1942 and left by the summer of 1943. These were 8 inch guns, built in early 1941. I've only found a few folks who actually saw them in place. One was Fred Eckenberg, brother of Henry, who was there when the gun was switched into the siding.

Here On the Home Front

USCG Station Ediz Hook

Commissioned in 1935, the USCG station on Ediz Hook was established to aid in anti-smuggling and law enforcement. During WWII, it played an important role in the defense of Clallam County both in the Strait of Juan de Fuca and along the Pacific coastal beaches. Reports of Japanese submarines were investigated by the crews stationed here in the Port Angeles area. It was also a base during the war to train aerial gunners. There was also a land rescue team stationed there. Navy pilots involved in plane crashes in this rugged Olympic Peninsula wilderness were rescued by these crews. Also it was here on Ediz Hook that Navy pilots trained for carrier landings by landing on a special short runway designed for just that purpose.

The following was published in the Peninsula Daily News column - Looking Back, 1938.

Survey work has begun on Ediz Hook for the Port Angeles Coast Guard Air Station's $96,000 landing field improvement project, said Lt. Cmdr. Norman M. Nelson, commanding officer. Engineer-in-charge W.I. Lippard, who directed a large part of the Clallam County Airport construction job in recent years, has a small Works Progress Administration crew working on the Hook. Two runways are to be constructed, and both will be lighted for night use, Nelson said. Currently, the air station has an unpaved emergency landing strip extending lengthwise on the Hook beside the station property.

It was September 1944 that the station officially became Coast Guard Group Port Angeles. By the end of that year, 29 aircraft had been assigned to the station. Also during WWII, the

Here On the Home Front

Air Station expanded to include a gunnery school training aerial gunners and local defense forces.

Fairchild Airport

The William R. Fairchild International Airport was developed beginning in 1934 by the U.S. Army, the U.S. Navy, and the Works Progress Administration and opened in 1937 serving as both a military and civilian airport. In 1948 it was named "Clallam County Municipal Landing Field" when turned over to the County. In 1951 it was transferred from the County to the Port of Port Angeles. The field was renamed William R. Fairchild International Airport in 1969 in honor of its first supervisor.

Jack Olson of Forks who was living in Port Angeles during the last part of the war remembered a P-38 hitting trees as they approached the airstrip where Lincoln Park is today.

John Jarvis of Agnew remembered the P-38's which were stationed there. "You would see P-38's and B-17 bombers flying over every day.

Merle Watson of Beaver who was attending Sequim school during the war also mentioned a P-38 crashing south of Sequim. He thought he had seen the pilot parachute out of the falling plane. This may have been an Army Air Corps P-38 Lightning that crashed in May of 1943. The pilot, however, was killed. The government shut down all the roads leading to the site.

This is not to be confused with the crash of a B-17 which occurred in 1952 near the Tubal Cane mine south of Sequim.

Cye Laramie and Glen Lane in 2002 found a Navy Avenger

Here On the Home Front

which had crashed in the upper Dungeness River area. The men had been searching for the crash site as it was Lane's uncle Leo Lane, a Navy aviator that was killed in the crash. Two other flyers were also killed. Cye and Glen placed a memorial plaque at the site of the 1944 crash.

Camp Hayden

Built in 1941 on approximately 500 acres at Tongue Point near Salt Creek west of Port Angeles, Camp Hayden was a WWII Coastal Artillery Camp. The Fort, first named "Striped Peak Military Reservation" was later named after Brigadier General John L. Hayden who was commanding officer of the Puget Sound harbor defenses.

Barracks were built along Salt Creek. About 150 soldiers were trained with many being shipped out of nearby Crescent Beach. Two large 16 inch guns were in place and it was said that the projectile could reach Vancouver Island approximately 18 miles across the Strait of Jan de Fuca. The guns could fire a one ton projectile almost 28 miles. Smaller 6 inch guns were also in place in the Batteries. Guns were also in place at Crescent Beach west of Hayden and Striped Peak. There was a kitchen and mess hall below ground as well as storage rooms. There were also power plants, observation and spotting stations, and early day radar systems along with a fire control station, post office, gymnasium, a theater and a wharf.

Beverly Porter of Joyce remembered she was attending Crescent High School when the war broke out and the road to Crescent Beach was closed to the public. "There was only one road to Crescent Beach at that time and it was closed immediately. That beach down there was our playground and we would even walk from home," said Beverly. Her home at that time was one mile south of what is now highway 112. Well the reason for the closure, you see, was that the government was building camp Hayden. "People such as the McFall family living near the beach were moved out of there. We could hear the dynamite going off and the percussion would shake our windows," said Beverly. Beverly also spoke of her brother-in-law Rusty Huff, Port Angeles manager for Tooker Freight based in Discovery Bay, who was driving freight truck picking up freight in Seattle bringing some of it out and Beverly's family found out when the camp was finally established that Rusty had been hauling equipment for camp Hayden.

June and John Nelson spoke of Camp Hayden. "Pneumonia Gulch" they called it, remarked Marge Deinis. "It was right down in a real damp part out there at Salt Creek."

"A lot of sickness?" I asked?

"Not really," said Marge, "but there were a lot of soldiers from the cities and some from much warmer and dryer climates not use to that type of weather and terrain in the winter. They were training soldiers there and shipping them out of Crescent Beach just west of Hayden."

Gordon Richards of Forks spoke of the guns there at Fort Hayden just after the war. Gordon was in the National Guard and spent a few weeks at Hayden training. The National Guard, which was established in June of 1933, was a part of the US Army which could be sent by the president of the United States into combat if needed. It has been said that approximately 300,000 men were brought into service by the National Guard just prior to the bombing of Pearl Harbor. The National Guard played a big role in battles such as Omaha Beach (D-Day) and Normandy.

The National Guard also was involved in an assault to remove Japanese forces from Manila. The National Guard had played a big role in the effort towards freedom during WWII.

When asked what kind of training Gordon was involved in at Camp Hayden Gordon responded, "Basically firing big guns. They still had 12 inch guns there and we had 90 mm guns we brought with us. We took target practice out towards the Straits. The 16 inch guns which could shoot 25 miles clear over to Vancouver Island had been removed before we arrived. I remember firing those 12 inch guns. Several of us would stand behind and when those guns went off you would roll right up on your toes and your mouth would be wide open. You had no control, you just did it. I remember they had an ambulance backed up there ten feet behind us and we were ten feet behind the gun. After the gun fired I turned around and the percussion had ripped all the insulation out of that ambulance."

Soldiers loading shells into the 16" guns in the bunkers at Camp Hayden. Photo from collection of Jack Zaccardo.

According to Gordon they always had this ambulance standing by when they fired the big guns. "Those 90 mm guns would fire 5 miles into the air and they used them for anti-aircraft. They shot 50 pound shells and could be set for whatever elevation you wanted them to explode," said Gordon. The guns were also used as anti-tank weapons.

The camp was abandoned by the U.S. Army in 1948 and declared surplus in 1949. Clallam County took over and soon developed the area as a park.

WWII in Clallam County

Camp Hayden's fortifications included 16 inch guns in concrete bunkers. Some of the bunkers remain at the Clallam County Park. Photo from collection of Jack Zaccardo.

Here On the Home Front

Lake Ozette and Beach Patrols

Located in the North West corner of Washington State was the wilderness area of Lake Ozette just a few short miles from the rugged Washington coast line. According to the writings of the War Diary Office, 13th Naval District United States Coast Guard, no other area in the country offered more disadvantages for patrols, particularly that portion on the western side of the Olympic Mountains, which form the backbone of the Olympic Peninsula. It was here one found one of the last primitive areas of the Northwest, an area covered with thick virgin forests whose undergrowth was practically impenetrable. The wild beaches were rocky and difficult to traverse. In some sections, the patrolmen would be obligated to climb and descend almost vertical walls. The many bays were separated by walls of rock which projected out to the sea, and the Coast Guardsmen in order to ascend and descend these obstacles had to use lines secured to boulders or trees atop the barriers.

On August 27, 1942 the 13th Naval District issued orders for a patrol to start operations in the Lake Ozette region by September 1. It was decided by the US military that the Coast Guard 'Would take over the Army camp and patrol duties at Lake Ozette. The Coast Guard was to use their own equipment and facilities for the purpose of maintaining a shore patrol in that vicinity and a coastal lookout at Cape Alava. It had already become apparent, and was proved conclusively later, that the theory of recruiting men in specific localities with minor physical disabilities was not a practical one, and, therefore, it was necessary to use regular Coast Guardsmen. The three days allotted was a short interval of time for the selection of the original complement and to assemble the necessary equipment and gear for the station.

The officers designated to organize the station knew in advance the harsh, strenuous life which faced the members of the patrol during the first few months, and they selected their men from the Big Four Receiving Station on a volunteer bases. Rigid qualifications were required of the men; they had to have a thorough knowledge of the woods and be willing and able to work fourteen hours each day, seven days a week, with no thought of liberty the first few months. They had to be good rifle shots, good cooks, good walkers and in other words, good all - around men.

The US Coast Guard men and equipment were assembled at the Seattle Repair Yard on September 1, 1942 and a convoy consisting of two large trucks, ·a carryall, and four privately-owned cars departed for the wilderness of Lake Ozette. Immediately upon the arrival of the Coast Guard, the army was officially relieved, and the Ozette Beach Patrol Base was formally established. The special clothing, pack boards, compasses, cooking utensils, and firearms were segregated into piles, and from them, the men outfitted themselves. Two parties of four men then departed for the beach that was a distance of three and one-half miles over forest trails. On their backs, they carried sleeping bags, water, food, cooking utensils, rifles, and ammunition; and in their minds, they carried no idea of what the future held in store for them here in the wilderness. Here at Ozette.

WWII in Clallam County

Upon arrival at the beach the two groups of men made camps. There were no quartering facilities of any kind, and the area was uninhabited. The men were getting the first taste of their new life, and during the first night, one man stood watch over his three mates who slept on the ground. Skunks, rats, and mice were everywhere, and occasionally a bear could be heard.

The first patrolmen covered approximately twelve miles of rocky coastline each day, prepared their own meals over campfires, and slept on the damp ground at night. After three days, two additional patrols were established which provided complete coverage twice a day of the twenty-six miles comprising the Lake Ozette section. Each patrol remained on the beach for a period of from two to sixteen days, depending upon the availability of the men.

After two weeks had passed, tents were put up at the five beach camps and trails opened through the dense forest to the camps. For about four months, the men continued to use campfires or old metal drums in place of stoves; and though the tents provided shelter, they contained no floors or frames.

The station proper was a busy place. The Coast Guard had taken over five one-room shacks and one old houseboat which were situated at the north end of the lake at the dead-end of a secondary road. The quartering facilities for the thirty men consisted of these shacks and the houseboat.

Folding army cots occupied all of the available floor space in each cabin, and forced each man to crawl over his shipmates' bunks in order to reach his own. The galley and mess hall consisted of one small service station building with a constantly smoking galley range. The combination office, storeroom, armory, radio room, and repair shop consisted of one small nine- by eighteen-foot shack.

The Coast Guard Beach Patrol at Lake Ozette constructed a camp including barracks, a mess hall, armory and other facilities supporting the patrol effort. Photo from Olympic National Park.

However, the men who composed the first complement at Lake Ozette were a resourceful clan. Together they set about building themselves a station. By Christmas, a 150 by 20 foot barracks building, a storeroom and armory, and other buildings were completed. Eighteen miles of forest trails had been opened up. By the end of the third month, the station pointed with pride to their first shower. All of the work was done by station personnel, and a period of three months quickly slipped by before any liberties or leaves were granted.

On the beaches lumber for the houses was towed in by raft form from Neah Bay. Every nail, tool, and utensil was carried in on the backs of men, and one stout fellow earned himself a reputation by carrying a 100 pound stove from Lake Ozette to the beach without stopping. All the stoves were packed in this manner by Coast Guardsmen.

During the construction of the station and shelter houses the Coast Guard Beach Patrols continued to guard the beaches. Training also continued as men were taught the care and use of the rifles, how to use natural cover to the best advantage, and how to approach unidentified individuals on the beach. A man who wore a camouflaged poncho and concealed himself in the shrubbery could not be seen at a distance of fifty yards.

Clothing for such duty as this was a constant source of trouble. The regulation clothing provided the men by the Coast Guard was insufficient and impractical. The rain clothing made of rubber lasted for no time at all and immediately became shreds once subjected to the snags of the forest. Regulation footwear was not sufficiently sturdy and proved very dangerous. What was actually needed were caulked boots which would not slip on the dry pine needles during the summer months and which would have a lasting quality when worn on the rocky beaches. The men purchased most of their clothing for use in the woods from a nearby logging outfit and had more the appearance of "timber beasts" than of Coast Guardsmen. Finally, Headquarters authorized the purchase and issuance of caulked boots and foul weather gear suitable for the work.

In October, 1942, approximately two months after the authorization of beach patrols, head-quarters requested the District Coast Guard Officer to furnish the number of dogs needed to establish sentry dog patrols on the coast. By December, Men from the 13th Naval District were sent to the War Dog Reception and Training Center in Fort Robinson, Nebraska. A total of 10 dog handlers and 40 dogs were soon assigned to the Lake Ozette area. There were also 3 handlers and 12 dogs assigned to Baadah Point in Neah Bay.

Two Coast Guard patrol boats were used for the distribution of personnel and for patrolling the lake. All of the trails connecting the lake and the beach did not end at the station, but merely at the shore of the lake. This system gave added security and relieved the need for further construction of trails through the wilderness. Also the Navy designated Lake Ozette as an emergency landing area, and during patrols, the Coast Guard was on alert for disabled planes.

Also according to a 13th Naval District history document beach patrolmen on a number of occasions provided valuable assistance after military planes had been forced down or made crash landings along the coast. In March of 1944, a Navy PBY flying boat was forced down on the south end of Lake Ozette.

One engine had completely failed and the other was showing

signs of quitting when the plane landed. Stranded helplessly on the lake, the plane was in grave danger of going aground. The CGR-1310 on routine patrol on that area of the lake at the time towed the plane to the mooring buoys in Swan Bay, a distance of approximately six miles from the site of the plane's landing.

March of 1944, a Navy PBY flying boat was forced down on the south end of Lake Ozette due to a failed engine. It was towed to Swan Bay where it was repaired. Photo from Forks Timber Museum, Dobbins Collection.

Here On the Home Front

Immediate investigation revealed that one engine had to be replaced and the other repaired. Personnel of the Coast Guard Beach Patrol Station, Ozette volunteered all possible assistance. Within fifteen minutes after the plane had been secured, Coast Guard personnel had furnished the Navy with a complete plan for replacing the 2,300 pound engine. The plan was gladly accepted by the Navy crew and placed into execution at once.

The Coast Guard telephone lines truck at Port Angeles furnished a pole derrick two days later to lift the engine from the truck and to lower it to a raft which was placed directly beneath the bridge crossing the Ozette River. The defective engine and propeller were lifted from the raft to the bridge and placed on the Navy truck. The raft transporting the new engine was towed by the CGR-1310 out of the Ozette River and across Ozette Lake to Swan Bay where the repairs were made by Coast Guard and Navy personnel. The entire operation was accomplished in about three days and the plane was capable of taking off from the lake under its own power.

By the end of 1942, Beach Patrols were also operating at Baadah Point in Neah Bay and also at La Push. Other Coast Guard outposts along the north coast were, Seafield, Ozette River, Cape Alava, Sand Point, Wink Trail, Yellow Banks, Allens Bay Trail, Eagle Point, and Starbuck.

Also in the early 40's a telephone spur line was installed from Sekiu to the Lake Ozette Headquarters and the Ozette Beach Patrol.

The Lake Ozette Beach Patrol Station was finally decommissioned on March 29, 1944, and one of the most colorful of the Coast Guard units in the Pacific Northwest ceased to operate here in Clallam County, Washington. *Here on the Home Front.*

Here On the Home Front

La Push Beach Patrol Station

According to the War Diary Office, USCG beach patrols stations were also located at La Push on the Quileute Indian Reservation and at Kalaloch. The Coast Guard station at La Push was commissioned 1 October, 1942. The La Push patrols were responsible for covering the beaches from Cape Johnson (north of La Push) to south of Hoh Head. Outpost camps were established at Mora, Third Beach, Mosquito Creek, and Toleak Point. It was here along this wilderness beach line that approximately twenty eight dogs helped to patrol the shoreline against any possible Japanese shore attack. Also as added protection the Coastal Lookout System maintained a lookout tower on James Island at the mouth of the Quillayute River and a light station on Destruction Island south of La Push. One of the most heroic events occurring in the La Push area during the war years was that of the USCG rescuing those aboard the Russian steamship Lamut on April 1, 1943. No April fool's joke. See Wreckage of the Lamut, page 233.

Here On the Home Front

Coast Guard Station in La Push, Washington on the Quileute Indian Reservation in 1970. Photo by Lonnie Archibald.

Naval Auxiliary Air Station, Quillayute

According to information acquired by Forks High school and UW graduate and historian Harvey Green it was nearly a year before the Japanese attacked Pearl Harbor, that tension between the U.S. and Japan heightened and the United States began a search for suitable sites to construct airfields. These fields would provide protection, and training facilities for the Armed Forces, should war occur. Construction was soon under way on a number of air bases throughout the 48 states and in the off shore territories. Of the many airfields constructed by the U.S. Army, Navy, Marines and Coast Guard, one airfield would stand out as the most difficult and challenging, the Quillayute Air Station. The only other readily usable site in the area was a municipal emergency field at the town of Forks. This site was found to small. In making his recommendation the Commanding Officer of Naval Air Stations pointed out that satisfactory gunnery area elsewhere were not available and that Quillayute might have tactical advantage in putting Squadrons aboard or taking them off carriers as they went to sea or returned through the Strait of Juan de Fuca.

First started by the U.S. Army, and later taken over by the U.S. Navy, the Naval Auxiliary Air Station, Quillayute was located on the Olympic Peninsula on the remote Quillayute Prairie, a short distance from the Pacific Ocean and the Native American Reservation at La Push, and approximately 10 miles west of Forks.

From this location, aircraft such as the Grumman F-4F

Here On the Home Front

Wildcat (Fighter aircraft), Grumman TBF Avenger (Torpedo bomber) and the later Grumman F-6F Hellcat (Fighter aircraft) could be flown to the aircraft carriers as they left the "Strait of Juan de Fuca and headed out to the Pacific Theater of War. Upon their return from duty, the above mentioned aircraft could be flown from the carriers to the Quillayute Air Base where they could be dispatched to their final destination.

The Quillayute Airbase from directly overhead, showing the aircraft parking, runway, taxiways, and buildings on the base. Photo from the Forks Timber Museum Dobbins Collection.

Preliminary negotiations for the purchase of property on the Quillayute Prairie were authorized in November 1940 and within eleven days a recommendation for the purchase of 520 acres at an estimated cost of $24,400 was returned to the Bureau of Aeronautics. On the same day, notice was given to the Clallam County Board of Commissioners that the Navy would not lease the emergency landing strip at Forks because of the lack of space for expansion, but would probably develop a new airfield on the Quillayute Prairie. Appraisals of the value of land to be purchased were completed in March 1941. Private appraisals placed a value of $19,075 on the 520 acres. The land was acquired on March 31, 1941. Field work began on May 2, 1941 by a private contractor, Austin Company. The amount allotted for Quillayute was $20,825.

The first development at Quillayute, completed on October 24, 1941 was a graded and graveled landing strip 300 feet wide and 4,290 feet long. There were no housing facilities but farm buildings left by the former owners were cited as available for remodeling to house 25 officers and 50 men. The airstrip was soon increased to one 6000 foot runway and two 5000 foot runways. At that time the base was a joint use facility by both Navy and Army personnel.

The station was built in 1943 to meet 1942 planning for protection against enemy air attacks, with housing units a mile and a half away from the hangar, gasoline storage tanks scattered around the perimeter of the field and some two miles of concrete taxiway.

Here On the Home Front

The Army, and later the Navy, worked under difficult conditions. Roads were few, narrow, and either just oiled or not surfaced at all. The nearest railroad connection was nine miles east from the base. This was a 60 mile logging spur from Port Angeles. All material had to be trucked in, either from the end of the railroad spur near what was later known as Kitchel's Reload or trucked in from such cities as Seattle, Bremerton and Port Angeles. Electric power had to be developed on the spot, water had to be supplied by digging wells and housing had to be provided for civilian workers as well as military personnel. Also there was a lack of workmen as many were recruited from distant places.

More information acquired by Harvey Green is as follows. The Army had a various times planned to build two or possibly three runways at the Quillayute Air Station, but the work completed at the time of turning it back to the Navy consisted of one concrete runway 150 feet wide and 5000 feet long with surrounding taxiways, hard standings, and parking area. The Army also completed a cantonment of 21 buildings in the extreme north west corner of the station which included a mess hall, dispensary, officers' quarters (50 men), heads, and barracks (400 men); strung 9 miles of power line; erected a 36,000 gallon water tank; partially fenced the station and constructed several small buildings for administration, shops, etc.

Official action leading to the relinquishing of Army improvements to Navy owned fields in the State of Washington began in October, 1943, when the Fourth Air Force notified the Pacific Division of the U.S. Engineers that no further new construction would be processed under the supervision of the Army. The Navy CO's of Quillayute made a request of permission to use Army buildings at Quillayute and the Commanding Officer, Army Air Commanding General, Fourth air Force, was notified of this action January 17, 1944, with the explanation that the Army would be enabled to withdraw its guard detachment. The change in the war situation was the reason for Army withdrawal from Navy bases. It was recommended that the Army facilities be transferred to the assignment and control of the Navy.

Official transfer of Army installations at Quillayute was not completed until December 18, 1944. The delay was apparently not a result of any desire of the Army to hold the installation, but rather resulted from efforts to clarify the Navy's plan for reimbursement to the Army for money expended.

Here On the Home Front

The Commissioning Ceremony

It was February 29, 1944 and what a grand day it was for a commissioning ceremony at the Naval Auxiliary Air Station Quillayute. Sunshine, bands, speakers and food enlighten all those who visited this wilderness Air Base. In attendance were Native American families from La Push, logging and farming families, school students, military commanders, Clallam County Commissioners, American Legion Auxiliary, a musical band from the Quillayute Union (Forks) High School, Base Commander Lieutenant Robert N. Dobbins, and Chaplain M. E. Smith who gave the invocation and benediction. It was estimated that 1,200 attended the ceremony, including approximately 800 civilians from the surrounding communities.

Dorothy Burr of Forks remembered playing her clarinet with the Forks High School Band during the dedication. She was only in the eighth grade but was asked to play with the high school students. Dorothy also remembered seeing the band's photo in the Seattle paper following the dedication. "I remembered how thrilled we were looking at the airplanes at Quillayute and thinking this is it, this is war," said Dorothy.

Here On the Home Front

Dorothy Burr of Forks who played during the Quillayute Airport commissioning ceremony while in the eighth grade now plays for the Forks City Orchestra. She is pictured here during the 2011 Forks 4th of July parade. Photo by Lonnie Archibald.

The Quillayute Naval Auxiliary Air Station commissioning ceremony on February 29, 1944 was attended by and estimated 1,200 people. Photo from the Dobbins Collection, Forks Timber Museum.

NAVAL AUXILIARY AIR STATION, QUILLAYUTE, IS COMMISSIONED

At public ceremonies, the Quillayute Naval Air Station was officially commissioned Tuesday afternoon at 2:00. Approximately 800 people from Forks, Beaver, Sappho, Tyee, Bogachiel, Port Angeles and vicinities witnessed the memorable scene.

The day was perfect for such an occasion. The sun overhead proudly shone down on the scene below displaying to advantage the air station nestled in the low foothills. Following the program, crowds were invited to inspect the station, including runways, buildings and grounds. Work has not yet been completed on landscaping of the grounds.

PLANES OVERHEAD

Previous to the afternoon's program, three patrol bombers flew overhead. Later in the day, a blimp passed over the airfield. Spectators also had an opportunity to see a Navy Transport plane and another plane take off from the field.

COMMISSIONING

Chaplain M. W. Smith opened the commissioning ceremonies with a short prayer. The authorization for commisssioning of the air station was then given by Commander John J. Berger, acting commandant, Naval Air Center, Seattle.

Lt. Robert N. Dobbins, commanding officer Naval Air Station, Quillayute, then read the orders. Following this, flag raising ceremonies took place while the Quillayute Union High School band played "The Star Spangled Banner." The armed guard detail presented arms and posted a guard.

Roy Atterberry, Sequim, chairman of the board of county commissioners, extended a greeting from the county to navy officers and their men.

Mrs. Beatrix Palmer, president of the American Legion Auxiliary at Forks, represented the Forks community. In her greeting, Mrs. Palmer said that she was highly honored to be chosen to welcome the Navy to Forks. She voiced the opinion of many when she said that people of this community will do all in their power to tender their hospitality toward men of the armed forces.

VISITING DIGNITARIES

Visiting Navy dignitaries at the commissioning ceremonies included:

Captain H. F. Gimgrich, supply officer, Naval Air Station, Seattle;

WWII in Clallam County

Remembering Quillayute

Johnny Leppell of Forks remembered when the Quillayute Air Base was being built in the 1940's that concrete was being shipped by railroad boxcars to a location near the La Push Road and Highway 101. The Navy hired high school kids and others to load the 94 pound sacks of concrete onto flatbed trucks. The heavy sacks were then hauled to Quillayute.

"Most of the men were working in the woods or had been drafted and there weren't many of us young men left in town to speak of. Most of the sand and gravel for mixing came off Rialto Beach," said John. There were a lot of blackberry vines growing all over Quillayute Prairie and according to John one of the jokes going around when they were building the runways was that they mixed in blackberry seeds so when the place was someday abandoned it would go back to nature like the land the Olympic National Park had taken from the homesteaders. John remembered that there were a lot of gravel trucks brought in from out of the area to work at the Airbase as back then there weren't that many trucks in the Forks area like there were in the 70's.

John also spoke of the old worn out power plants that the military brought into Quillayute. It took a lot of labor to keep them running. Big Bertha and Dirty Dora were names given to those almost worthless power plants.

COCKROACHES FROM QUILLAYUTE. John also spoke of the war years when he was helping the Forks Creamery, which at that time was located along what is now Calawah Way and Spartan Avenue. According to Jim Klahn, the Forks and Port Angeles Creameries had merged in 1938. Anyway getting back to what it was John said, "I weighed in the milk, pasteurized and bottled it all illegally. You were supposed to have a license to-do this. There were no men around except for one older farmer who helped. Anyway, we started getting cockroaches in Forks and we had never had them in town before WWII," said John.

Marge Cowan-Jensen of Beaver also remembered Cockroaches. "My Uncle Raleigh Konopaski hauled produce to Forks from Clallam Bay and they were especially in the banana crates," said Marge.

So where were they coming from, John wondered. One day the milk truck came back from its delivery at the Quillayute Air Base with boxes of empty milk bottles. "They backed the truck up to the back door to unload and here were all these cockroaches running all over the place. The creamery guys were bringing them to Forks in the milk boxes from the Air Base," said John. Who knew how they got to the Base but probably from some goods or equipment delivered from the southeastern states. And so it was, the creamery became a distributorship for more than just milk. They had unknowingly been transporting the not so famous Quillayute Air Base cockroaches to local stores by way of their milk deliveries. John said he latter made the trip to the Base and saw the critters moving about on the bulletin board and even in the kitchen where steam kettles were being used for cooking. "The Navy must have learned to live with the cockroaches because they sure had them," said John. Walt

Fuhrman of Forks remembered loggers racing cockroaches on the bar at the Evergreen Cafe in Forks. "I guess there were no ration stamps needed. They came free to the Customers, you see," said Walt.

Darrell Klahn of Forks recalled during the war the Forks High School classes getting smaller as some of the guys ahead of him were ready to go into the military and they did so. Darrell thought the military would take students down to the age of 17. They got credited for leaving high school to go into the service," said John Leppell. Darrell remembered working at the Quillayute air Base when he was a sophomore in high school. "I got extra gas for my dad's car because I carried others to work down there," said Darrell. He had to apply for a special gas ration sticker in order to receive the extra fuel. Darrell's job at the airport was to dig deep holes down below the hill south of the airport in search of the proper mixture of gravel they needed to mix with the cement for the runways.

Maynard Lucken of Beaver also worked at the Airport in early 45 building a bomb shelter and storage units when the war ended.

Ron Shearer remembered the concrete at the Quillayute Air base runways being very thick. "Some of the gravel came in by barge up the Quillayute River at high tide. They would tie up and unload it there at Rialto Beach where the parking lot is now. I believe some of the gravel came from that area as well," said Ron.

Here On the Home Front

Jack Olson of Forks, who during the starting of the war, lived at Mora near where the ONP Ranger Station sits today remembered the gravel being hauled off Rialto Beach to the airport by old six wheel Ford trucks that were chain driven. "One winter the roads all froze up and then in the spring it thawed out. And that was a mess. They had to build a plank road on one side of the road part way between Rialto Beach and Richwine Road. I used to watch those trucks get stuck in the mud. They would break a chain and the driver would have to crawl under the truck to make repairs." said Jack.

Pat (Blevins) Mansfield of Forks also shared memories of the Quillayute Airport. "My mother and stepfather and I went there one time and after dad answered several questions given by the two white clothed sailors at the gate we drove on through. I was so amazed at ever seeing such a tall building as the lookout tower and there were several planes on the runway and they had their motors running and there was a lot of noise. Of course I was pretty young but it seemed to me like there were hundreds of men marching around in white uniforms and there were new buildings everywhere. It was a busy place. It was awesome."

Art Anderson said that one time he went out there when they were building those runways and if the ground wasn't level they would just fill it full of cement. "There were places out there where the runways were 6 to 10 feet deep with cement," said Art.

GOOSE DINNERS. John Leppell told a story about Goose dinners. The Quillayute Prairie was on the flyway for geese heading south for the winter and north for the summer and the feathered aircraft often lit in the fields throughout the prairie. Soon after the first cement runway was constructed at the Air Base geese would come in trying to land on what they thought was water. After a rain the lights from the hangers shining on the cement runway made it appear as water and the geese were killing themselves hitting so hard. "They had sort of emergency goose dinners at the Navy Base after those hard landings," said John. On one occasion 62 geese were brought in on one afternoon for a special Halloween dinner for the entire mess. Fresh crab and salmon from La Push, trout from the rivers, bear meat, elk meat, venison and ducks also complimented dinners from time to time here on this wilderness Naval Base.

ROUGH ROADS. John and Darrell spoke of the tough times Clallam County road crews had keeping the graveled road maintained from the Highway 101 junction to the Air Base as there was a lot of traffic trucking in supplies. The curvy road would turn to mud when it rained. The same stood true of the road west from the Air Base to Rialto Beach. "They were hauling gravel off Rialto Beach. You could get gravel right out of the river and off the beach in those days," said Darrell. Darrell also remembered trucking special cut lumber from the Carlsborg Mill to the Air Base.

BUZZING QUILLAYUTE UNION HIGH SCHOOL. Darrell also backed the story that Lawrence Gaydeski had shared of a Navy Plane from the Quillayute Air Base buzzing the High School. "I saw him coming from the Quillayute area and those airplanes had big round radial engines on 'em and they made a strange sound; kind of a distinctive roar to it that you could identify as that of a

Here On the Home Front

Wildcat and that is what they were using out there. He came straight for the high school. He never missed it by much and sure enough they got his plane number and he was soon gone from the Base," said Darrell. Gaydeski mentioned that the plane had circled from the east and actually flew under the power lines. The next morning the pilot's High school student girlfriend came to class with tears in her eyes as her "fly boy pilot" had been shipped out.

John Leppell told of the planes coming in from Quillayute and circling above the hills on the upper Calawah River then flying near the school in route to the rocket range which was just west of town and north of what today is the Dahlgren place along Bogachiel Way.

Myron Simmons remembered gravel trucks running all night long when building the runways. Out across from where the hanger is today was a great big pit where we dumped all the rocks that we took off between the runways. Over in the north east corner clear across all the runways and everything as you go down towards Colby Creek was an Army Base and they had a hospital, barracks, a mess hall and everything," said Myron. Myron also remembered that the gate to the Air Base was located west of the Quillayute cemetery. There were two officers' houses just west of the cemetery; one was where Commander Dobson lived.

AN AIRPLANE MECHANIC. Fred Shaw of Forks graduated from high school at the age of 17 in 1939 in McCleary, Washington. He joined the Navy in 1941 wanting to be an aircraft mechanic.

Fred had loved to mechanic on the farm and was interested in WWII aircraft. After taking flight lessons Fred was stationed at Sand Point, Idaho when the Navy in 1944 sent him to Quillayute where he would work on Grumman "Hellcat" planes along with P 38's and other models. "On the job training," said Fred. Fred remembered planes running torpedo and bombing practices off La Push with an island being the target. Fred also mentioned a young pilot crashing at Kalaloch on March 22, 1944 and also a plane crashing at Quillayute damaging the engine in which Fred latter repaired. He did his plane repairs in the large hanger which still exists today. The Kalaloch crash was a B-25 Bomber in which no one was injured but the plane was lost.

Here On the Home Front

A crew responds to an airplane crash at Quillayute that resulted in a damaged prop and engine. Photo from the Forks Timber Museum, Dobbins Collection.

Power Plants

John Leppell spoke of the old worn out power plants that had been brought in to the Base. The equipment built in 1916 was used for more than a quarter of a century in the town of Casper, Wyoming. It's been said that as soon as these bulky antiques arrived at the Air Station for assembling it was apparent that they were going to be a source of continuing trouble and that they were. It was a constant battle to keep the diesel generators running. Big Bertha and Dirty Dora were the names given to those two miserable power plants.

Large diesel powered electrical generators of 1916 vintage proved to be unreliable and a maintenance and operation problem.
Photo from the Forks Timber Museum, Dobbins Collection.

Here On the Home Front

Another plane mishap which did not turn out as fortunate for the pilot was that of two planes colliding when flying side by side just a few miles off of Destruction Island. Grover Consford had taken off from the Quillayute Airbase on a September morning flying south west of Quillayute when he collided with wing mate Dwight Cochehour. Both men managed to parachute out of their planes but Consford was injured and was never able to inflate his life raft. A crash boat picked up Cochehour but there was no sign of Consford. A memorial service was held that October for the missing naval pilot.

Frances Maxfield, who lived with her husband Art on the Maxfield homestead on the east side of the Mina Smith Road just east of the Quillayute Airbase remembered the old plane lookout tower on her farm there on the prairie. After the war when it was torn down they used the building for a bus stop for the kids who attended school in Forks.

Ron Shearer remembered going down to the Quillayute Airbase with his dad at night on the gas truck and seeing clusters of lights here and there where construction companies were busy setting up camps and working on their equipment as the base was being built. The roads at the base were mud at that time. "Dad would flash his lights when stuck and a cat would come pull him to where he was to dump fuel then back to the road again and dad would make the trip back to Forks for another load. This could go on all night long. I remember going down there once and there must have been a hundred International dump trucks are lined up ready to haul gravel. All the black dirt had to be removed then gravel had to be laid for a base before the concrete could be poured," Said Ron

Joelene (Goodie) Wittenborn remembered working at Quillayute during the summer when the Base was being built. "I waited tables for the work crews that were doing the construction. I also worked in the restaurant when the Base was commissioned in February of 1944. There were trailers for those who worked there so I stayed right there."

The Wittenborns remembered that when the Base was being built the old road to Quillayute was graveled, narrow, and curvy with lots of stumps. Almost a one lane road and was very dangerous. "You had to be drunk to drive it," said Joelene's husband Ernie. Later after the base was complete the road was fixed up. There had been several serious accidents there along that wilderness road you see.

Ed Duncan who lived on the Little Quillayute Prairie during the war remembered all the planes coming and going and the soldiers living in the old Quillayute Store and school gym. He also remembered the Quonset huts and underground buildings where ammunition was stored. Ed also spoke of the blimp that crashed and a friend of his folk's that was hurt in that incident. The blimp crashed just a short distance from the airport.

Ed also spoke of the Liberty bus, which held 32 passengers, and would take the military and civilian workers back and forth from the Airbase to Forks. "You would practice every night at Quillayute Union High School (known as Forks High School today) for basketball and football and have to walk home from

Here On the Home Front

Forks to Quillayute and the Liberty Bus would just pass you by. After games Ed would also have to walk home. A distance of about 13 miles in my estimation.

Bert Fletcher remembered his mother having a pass to the Quillayute Air Base as Bert's father, Henry Fletcher was a Navy Petty officer in the South Pacific. Bert during the summer months would go along with his mom to the base. "We knew a half a dozen different sailors out there and one of them would pick me up from her and take me out and let me look at all the airplanes. I remember one time they took me clear out to the runway where the planes had just landed and they would taxi by and the pilots would wave at me and I was just thrilled to death. I was 8 or 9 years old then and highly interested in airplanes.

Jack Olson of Forks remembered while living at Mora as a kid he and his dad Jack would fish for salmon off La Push. "My dad had a fishing boat during the first part of the war after the ONP took the land and I would go out there fishing with him. We would go out at 5 a.m. At times dive bombers would be bombing them rocks out there but we never seen them. The USCG would let us know where and when the bombing would take place," said Jack.

Some of the salmon you caught near where the bombing took place would have jelly type eggs when opened and Jack thought it was because of the bombing. "We ate fish livers back then," said Jack.

"Riding the school bus home from Forks to Mora we went

through the airport and these planes were right beside the school bus trying to get into a close formation up behind each other and this one pilot came up behind this other guy and chewed his tail off with the prop," said Jack.

Walt Fuhrman of Forks was only 13 when he and Gene Foster went down to the Quillayute Airport to hit them up for a summer job. Gene could drive. "We went down and talked to this contractor, he was putting in runway lights about six by ten feet wide and thirty inches deep. I think the guys name was Bill Kerschner and he had a 1941 Dodge truck and he asked, "can you drive?" and I said, "heck yes I can drive." He said, "drive me around the block," and so I drove him around the darn block and the only thing I had ever driven was the old man's old Buick truck to spread fertilizer on the garden and I could only move it about six feet at a time. Anyway I made the grade and he said when it was time to haul cement for the lights I could drive and that was ok with me," said Walt. When driving truck Walt would drive up to the runway and look up at the light. "When I got the green light I could drive out onto the runway and up to get a load of cement. Coming back with a load it was the same procedure waiting for the green light," said Walt. During the war they were hard up for drivers. In between hauling cement Walt, Gene Foster, Gene's nephew, and Harry Hagadorn dug holes for the installation of the runway lights.

"I found out that if I wore a sailor's hat and bell bottom trousers I could eat at the mess hall for nothing but one day when I came to work I had to check in with the guard up by the cemetery and they took away my hat and then I had to pay for

Here On the Home Front

my food," said Walt.

"One time the Grumman Wildcat planes had all taken off and I had gotten the green light to drive out onto the runway and all of a sudden I heard a whoosh go over head and saw a Grumman Hellcat whose motor had conked out go right over my truck. It lit just the other side of me and scared the heck of out me," said Walt. Walt also told about the time he and Harry Hagadorn were working out where the short and the long runways intersect. "Here came this bomber with one wheel down and one up so he got the red light and circled to come in again and this time he had the opposite wheels up and down. He got the red light again and up he went," said Walt.

"He came around again and this time both wheels were up and the prop was hitting the runway going clank, clank, and screeching and us like a bunch of dumb bunnies just stood there watching it go by just twenty feet away," said Walt. Walt and Harry then watched the crews load the plane up and haul it away. "An ambulance came out but no one was hurt," said Walt.

Walt also remembered a few years after the war finding a Grumman Wildcat out on the Dickey on the back side of the airport while working for Frontier Logging. "We took a dump truck out there and loaded the motor up and Jack James hauled it off someplace, I don't know where," said Walt.

Bert Fletcher mentioned, "The main mission at Quillayute was ground attack refresher training. Pilots that may have done a tour of duty, as I understood it, would come to Quillayute and have his flying skills refurbished. They had a big school there with six or eight class rooms with blackboards for pilots." Bert also remembered the planes as they came screaming over Forks a mile apart coming from the north then turning heading west towards the rocket range. "It was constant," said Bert.

Bert also mentioned that his mother Estene was at one time president of the Petty Officer's Wives Club at the Base. They would have meetings once a month out there and she would either take the Liberty bus or drive her 1930 black 4 door Buick Marquette sedan which was in production from 1929 to 1931. The Base sailors were always after her to sell it. They would buy a car then sell it to other sailors when they got transferred from the Base.

Bert also remembered the restaurant fountain. "That was the first time I ever had a strawberry Sunday and man I thought that was just terrific," said Bert.

George Early of Clallam Bay remembered working at the Quillayute Airbase when it was being built. George was 16 and living in Forks at the time and would ride to work with some of the gravel truck drivers and sometimes the officers. "I worked as a carpenter and there were various things to do you see. It was early 1942, I think, and they were getting ready to move the first squadron in and a lot of the work was top secret stuff. I worked there into 1944. You couldn't say anything about what was being done there. The old runway had been torn up and work was being done on new ones," said George.

Here On the Home Front

George remembered when some of the first planes were brought in and they were training pilots. George remembered the Hellcats and Wildcats. Mostly carrier planes and there were bombs stacked up there.

"A lot of the buildings and barracks had three roofs on them. They were hot tarred and they put gravel from Rialto Beach on the tar. Sometimes three coatings. It would stand up better against bullets in case of an attack," said George.

He also remembered later years while working for the State Highway hauling gravel to the Air Base from the old pit which is located across from the weigh station at the north end of Forks. They soon had George running grader after that.

"They also had me move into the big hanger to hold a fire extinguisher when they worked on the two big power plant diesel engines. The foreman said they could easily catch on fire. I believe they finally blew them up with dynamite," said George. From the description given by George I believe those power plants to be the not so loveable Air Base power plants known as Big Bertha and Dirty Dora. So going on what George had described I guess they finally got what they deserved. A few sticks of dynamite.

Ruth (Dankert) Zinter and Dorothy (Dankert) Barker remembered while attending grade school at Quillayute along the Mina Smith road just a short distance from the Quillayute Air Base how the officers would come over to the school and the kids would serve them coffee. The men also invited the children to visit the airbase where they could look over all the airplanes.

This was prior to the bombing of Pearl Harbor when the Army was stationed there. "We could look in the planes but couldn't go in any of them," said Ruth. There were a lot of planes including the B-29 Superfortress.

The ladies also remembered the day the Quillayute School burned down in December of 1941. There were about 30 children attending the school back then and they were having their Christmas party and a play when Joe Wentworth, who was there at the time came, in and said "everybody out." "They told us we were going to see Santa Claus," said Dorothy.

The ladies remembered Daisy (Smith) Sinnema bringing a doll collection to school and it was destroyed in the fire. The school burned completely down and they had to finish the school year in the gym.

The following year the Quillayute children were transferred to the Quillayute Union School in Forks. They were bused from Quillayute Prairie over graveled roads to Forks.

Eddy Maupin was also attending school there on the Quillayute when the school burned. "I remember I was in the sixth grade and was to play the North Wind in the Christmas play and my mother made a special hat with a peaked top and a blue cape but I never got to use it because the school burned down. We had a half basement under the school with a big furnace. The pipe went under the school before turning up towards the chimney and there was a hole in the pipe and eventually the joist caught fire under there but thank goodness Joe Wentworth was right there to catch the fire but there was nothing he could do about it, it was too late. Well the school burned with the exception of the gym and an outbuilding. The gym, during a two week Christmas break, was remodeled with two class rooms and a third room where we could go and get warmed by the big old heater. It was sure a sorry day to see that little country school go." said Eddy.

The Quillayute School burned during the war. This photo shows the gymnasium building in 1979. Photo by Lonnie Archibald.

WWII In Clallam County

Quillayute School Fire

The following news article was provided by the Clallam County historical Society from an article written on December 17, 1941 in the Peninsula Evening News of Port Angeles

WEST END SCHOOL TOTAL LOSS AFTER UNEXPLAINED FIRE:

Fire of unexplained origin broke out in Quillayute Grade School, 12 miles from Forks, Wednesday night during a school Christmas program and totally destroyed the brick building.

The crowd of over a hundred children and adults attending the entertainment were marched from the building in good order and no one was injured but the building is a total loss, reports Deputy Sheriff W. M. Holenstein of Forks. There was $7,000 insurance on the building but the loss will be far greater. In addition to the building. 100 cords of wood and the fine shrubbery around the building were lost. Holenstein said.

The Forks, fire department, assisted by a great number of soldiers now stationed in Forks, arrived at the scene in time to save the Gymnasium, garage and light plant.

Forks Fire Chief Russell Vedder praised the soldiers for their fine work in fighting the fire. He said his department was considerably hampered in its work by lack of water and had to rely on chemicals to put out the blaze. The fire probably originated in the school basement, either from spontaneous combustion or from rain- soaked clothing which had been hung near the furnace to dry while the children attended the festivities upstairs Vedder said.

Soldiers remained on guard at the wreckage after the fire department members left.

Quick thinking on the part of teachers prevented any panic in clearing the building, witnesses said. The children were told they were going to

Here On the Home Front

see Santa Claus but would have to get up quietly and walk outside to see him. The building was emptied in good order without panic.

Blimp Crash at Quillayute

During WWII, blimps stationed in Tillamook, Oregon were used for anti-submarine and search patrol. Darrell Klahn told of a blimp that came to Quillayute during a storm and they had to try and get that thing tied down to the mooring post. "It was flip flopping around and I'm not sure but it seems like the men were trying to hold it down with their weight and one person fell and was injured," said Darrell. Fred Shaw, base airplane mechanic; stated that he was there but knew he would be in trouble if any of his crew were hurt in an attempt to stabilize the blimp. "It was thrashing about and when it hit the ground the engines were knocked out. The blimp finally hit timber a ways across the Little Prairie Road," said Darrell. And so Blimp K-39 was destroyed.

This occurred on January 4, 1944. It had attempted to make an emergency landing and to use the mooring mast which had been assembled. Several unsuccessful tries at a landing were made, but the wind finally carried the ship away and it crashed in the trees about a mile north of the station. The Blimp was a total loss. There were no fatalities but a number of serious injuries. Harvey Green spoke with Mr. William Noblette, who was the radio operator on the blimp. "He had been carried aloft and in dropping back to earth landed in the mud fracturing his back. His trip from Quillayute to the Port Angeles Hospital was one of his most vivid recollections of his wartime experiences. According to Mr. Noblette, who later lived in Ventura, California, "two drunk sailors" drove him into Port Angels over the very narrow, winding and unimproved roads," said Harvey.

Here On the Home Front

Wreckage of a blimp crash north of the Quillayute Naval Auxiliary Air Station. Photo from the Don Kaiser Collection.

Wreckage of the January 4, 1944 blimp crash north of the Quillayute Naval Auxiliary Air Station. Photo from the Don Kaiser Collection.

Wreckage of the January 4, 1944 blimp crash north of the Quillayute Naval Auxiliary Air Station. Photo from the Don Kaiser Collection.

On February 6, 1945 another blimp made an emergency landing at Quillayute. The landing crew soon had the blimp secured to the mooring mast and the Lighter-than-air ship was safe from the storm. It departed on more favorable weather conditions on February 8, 1945 for its home base in Tillamook, Oregon.

In another incident on June 5, 1945 a Tillamook based blimp, which had been moved to Quillayute, crashed while searching for a lost plane of the Royal Canadian Air Force in British Columbia. No one was injured.

Bert Fletcher claims that Quillayute had winds clocked as high as 90 miles an hour during the war.

George Early of Clallam Bay also had his recollection of the blimp crash. "It was storming to beat heck, you know how the wind blows out there. Anyway one of the Navy bosses and a foreman and I had just finished eating lunch and this one blimp came in and he was having just one heck of a time. He got down to the ground and they still had several contractors working around there and the men went down to the other end of the runway to get the spider to fasten down the blimp and half way up the runway the spider ran out of gas. Someone had siphoned the gas out you see and by that time the blimp was just all over the place. Anyway we walked over there and a lot of the contractors were there and one said they could go get one of the cherry pickers, which they did, and fastened onto the blimp and men were trying to hold the blimp down with lines and it was thrashing around and hit the ground breaking off one of the engines. Then it got loose and ended up hitting a big snag a ways from the landing site. One of the men said when it hit the ground to stay away from it because it was carrying 5 submarine bombs," said George. The blimp was destroyed.

Here On the Home Front

Blimps were deployed from their base at Tillamook, Oregon for patrols of the coast and used the Quillayute base. Photo from the Forks Timber Museum, Dobbins Collection.

WWII In Clallam County

Quillayute Quill

In an attempt to stimulate interest in old fashioned recreational possibilities and to build morale in the wilderness The "Quillayute Quill" was born. This was a newspaper of sorts published on base at the Quillayute Naval Base. After being approved by the Secretary of the Navy the six page announcement sheet and sports letter was published. A portion of one of these fine "Quill" issues passed down from Estene Fletcher and given to me by Bert Fletcher is shown here.

Here On the Home Front

INDEPENDENCE DAY SMOKER THRILLS HOLIDAY CROWD AT FORKS

Hard, fast, clean boxing and wrestling was exhibited to townspeople and naval personnel at the American Legion Arena, Tuesday evening, free of charge. Sponsored by the Quillayute Physical Training and Recreation Department, the show attracted approximately 700 patrons and proved a thriller from start to finish.

In the double main events, leather was thrown from every angle when the judges tallies were all counted, it was found "Brown Bomber" Bradshaw and "Kid Blitz" Tesnow had copped the dukes by unanimous decisions. Bradshaw, a former middleweight champion of Weco, Texas was hard pressed by "Lucky" Miller, of Brooklyn in the fastest and most spine tingling affair on the card. However T-Bone's slashing right gained the favor of the judges. Miller's stand was heroic and classy. Long cheers went up for both boys as they left the arena.

Tesnow's decision over "Slugger" Kelso was 2 rounds to 1, all through the ballots. The Kid's speed and boxing ability gave him the needed points to top the Fork's heavy who gave a game performance and was throwing more leather than his conqueror at the bell.

In the opener, Tommy Riggin, Aircrewman from Boys Town Nebraska, drew with Leonard Palmer, the hot drummer from Forks in a welter match. Both contestants showed class and the judges split.

Bout Two, saw Harold Mathey, Navy, cop a technical decision as Simmons, of Forks, fractured a thumb in a torrid mix-up at the close of Round 1. At this point the bout was even and had promise of being one of the cleverest bouts on the card.

Following the main event, an added attraction took place when "Shutterbug" Duffy, Navy, replaced Stevens from the Queets Ranger Station (whose duties made it impossible for him to show). His opponent was "Pink Lady" Hunt, who acquired a beautiful pair of pink lace women's apparel for his boxing trunks. Much to the delight of the large crowd gathered, a classy, fast bout ensued with both boys coming up with some good licks. Contest was ruled a draw.

On the wrestling card appeared a draw main; with "Gunner" Underwood, Chicago Technical Training Lightheavy and "Butcher" MacHugh, Washington State Heavyweight. The bout was slow and scientific as both boys countered quickly and failed to give the other any advantages. Every method was to attempt to determine a winner, but the affair proved a standoff.

In the other match, Bill Hyde, Alhambra City Middie, pinned Wild Willie Wells twice with body presses in 2:19 and 2:24.

Judges for the matches were Chaplain O'Brien, Navy, and Eddie Fox and Til Anderson of the American Legion. Referee duties were split between Promoters Millsap and Brauns of the Athletic Department.

NAVY COPS HOLIDAY TUG-O'-WAR AND $25 PRIZE MONEY

As part of the track and field entertainment, a tug-o'-war between "Loggers" and "Bluejackets" was won by the Navy musclemen and the prize of $25 went to Chief Doughty and his gang of tough hombres. Also winning prize money of $3 was a certain Ensign who removed his shoes and stockings and won the open 100 yard dash barefooted. We wouldn't give the secret away, however, he tries to sell War Bonds at the Rec. Hall.

QUILLAYUTE TOPS MERCHANTS IN SOFTBALL 13-4

Bluejackets of the Air Station hammered Forks pitching for a 13-4 victory in the early afternoon, July 4. Five spots in the Navy line up was filled by Colored Steward's Mates who gave a good account of themselves in the fielding and at the plate:

Box Score	Runs	Hits	Errors
Indians	13	12	3
Merchants	4	6	4

Tuffy and Taffy

There was a time when two cub bears, "Tuffy" and "Taffy" were presented to the Base by area citizens as mascots. The squadron named theirs "Tuffy" because of his unquenchable belligerency and his delight in biting the hands that fed him. The station named its mascot "Taffy" because he was sweeter than "Tuffy" but still hard to handle until warmed up to. Both mascots had short terms at the Base, however, as "Tuffy was thought to have jumped ship, enlisting in the Coast Guard as a bear cub of the same size, species, and disposition showed up at the USCG Base Ediz Hook in Port Angeles by coincidence at the time of the bears disappearance from Quillayute. "Taffy" sadly was killed when he fell from a tree at the Base.

Here On the Home Front

Tuffy and Taffy are introduced to the Quillayute Naval Auxiliary Air Station as mascots to the organization. Photo from the Dobbins Collection, Forks Timber Museum.

Liberty Bus

Transportation from the Quillayute Naval Air Station to Forks and Highway 101 was poor at best. When commissioned on February 29, 1944 the Base had one bus seating 32 men. This one bus was the only public transportation of any kind connecting with Forks. On Friday and Saturday nights the men would go into Forks 150 strong, and would stay until the beer taverns closed at midnight. Then they would all want to go back to the Base and those left in town waiting for 1 to 3 hours for the bus to return would usually stir up trouble of some kind or another to keep them amused. Not so amusing to law enforcement, however.

On April 25, a further request was made for additional busses on the basis of trouble developing in the logging town of Forks. On May 9 the request was repeated and a second bus arrived on May 13. As many Forks residents had mentioned, this wilderness town also offered dancing, roller skating, boxing and wrestling matches, tug-a-war's, baseball, basketball, and football games, a movie theater, etc., to those who wished to venture there.

Here On the Home Front

Rocket Range

John Leppell spoke of the fire on the Rocket Range on the north side of what today is Bogachiel Way west of Forks. The land which is located across Bogachiel Way from what today is the Joe Dahlgren place was being logged to be used by the Navy as a practice range. A fire broke out after the land was logged and helped by a strong wind it was actually threatening the town of Forks. "The funny part of it was when an article came out in the Seattle paper it read, "Fire rages on the Olympic Peninsula but they think they can save La Push." The wind was blowing the fire in an easterly direction and of course wouldn't have threatened La Push 12 miles west of Forks," said John.

It was Squadron VC-82's term in June 1945 that the fire broke out while land was being cleared for the rocket range. A fire permit had been issued to burn stumps in the range area. Dry weather and a brisk wind put the fire out of control and all hands became fire fighters. The blaze covered 600 acres of logged land and threatened a valuable stand of green timber. By trucks and planes men from the Naval Air Stations at Whidbey Island, Shelton, Port Angeles, Arlington and Seattle came to man fire trucks, hose lines, grub hoes, shovels, pump cans, walkie-talkies and even bulldozers. This fire became tough duty for all those who had gathered there. The Coast Guard also sent needed equipment from La Push, Neah Bay, Port Angeles, and the Army sent a detail of men from Ruby Beach.

By July 12th the fire was pretty much out. Watching from the school playground in Forks, Bert Fletcher remembered seeing a

Here On the Home Front

big Navy amphibian plane (Grumman Duck) circling and spotting fires and radioing them to ground personnel.

Ron Shearer remembered the rocket range once the Navy began using it for practice. "Those dive bombers would come in and sighted in on a round wood target which stood six feet in the air and maybe 60 yards across with a painted circle in the center and another circle inside that which was the bulls-eye. Planes would come in with little cast metal bombs which contained a plunger and white powder so they could see where the bombs hit. The planes would come in from Quillayute and circle the Calawah then fly right over Forks really pouring the coal to the engines. They would only be about 300 feet in the air and those engines really made a lot of noise," said Ron.

Grumman J2F1 amphibious plane of the type reported spotting for the forest fire operation

Here On the Home Front

Housing

In June of 1944 the Commanding Officer of Quillayute made a request for more substantial housing. On September 16, 1944, the Housing authority of Clallam County notified the Air Base that housing units had been approved for construction in Forks. On October 4, funds were being provided by the Navy for construction by the National Housing Agency. Also in October a request for 34 living units, laundry and storage units was made and approved.

Myron Simmons moved to Forks from Olympia during the war as his step father worked at Sappho Camp for Bloedel Donovan. There was a housing shortage in Forks during the war and the U.S. Government was at the time building housing projects in this frontier logging town. Myron remembered moving into the old Gray Projects on the south side of Calawah Way on the east side of Forks. "My step-father was exempt from the draft as he was a logger." said Myron. According to Myron the Gray projects was part of the logger's exemption plan. He remembered Jack Frost as the manager. When Myron married Jackie Kelm they also were able to move into those apartments. After the war the old office for the original Gray Projects was given to the Forks area VFW and moved down town and then later moved to George Campbell's property on the west side of town where his Forks Sand and Gravel was located. The building is still standing there today where it was used as the company's office.

Here On the Home Front

Forks Sand and Gravel office building in 2012. Photo by Lonnie Archibald.

In Port Angeles in 1943 housing known as "Mt Pleasant View" was built along Lauridsen Boulevard. Joe Blomgren of Forks also mentioned the four projects he remembered in Forks built during the war such as the Pink, Gray, Wood and Circle all on the east end of town. "Each apartment had about 20 units and they were primarily for the Navy personnel out at Quillayute," said Joe.

Bert Fletcher also mentioned how the town really grew during the war. He also mentioned the Pink Projects which were built in 1944 and located on the west side of what today is Fir Avenue, the Circle Projects on the north side of East Division Street across from where the Oscar Peterson place is today and two more projects along the south side of Calawah Way near what today is Maple Avenue . Bert also mentioned a trailer court on the south side of Calawah Way just west of the cemetery where several 24 foot RV trailers were situated in a big open field which contained a central community restroom.

Many of these projects and the RV spots were set up for Navy officers and pilots. Bert's mother, Estene, being a Navy wife herself opened up her home to the GI's and spent much time visiting the families there in Forks and on the Quillayute Naval Air Base. Bert also remembered Jack Frost as the maintenance man for many of the housing projects. Bert mentioned that when he came back home to Forks in 1959 that all were gone with the exception of the Circle and Pink projects.

I remember, when moving to Forks from Sequim in 1957, living next door to the Pink Projects and playing "Anti-I-Over" with several friends who lived there in the two story building. At that time the families were mostly those of loggers.

Bert also remembered Stucco houses owned by Bulla and Avery Holland of Forks and were situated on the west side of town. One long line of them was located just a block west of what is now Forks Avenue. Navy personnel also lived there during the war.

Here On the Home Front

Japanese Paper Balloon Bombs

THE MITCHELL MONUMENT. On May 5, 1945 in the backwoods and meadows of Gearhart Mountain near Bly in Southern Oregon an Alliance Church group was on a picnic when they came upon a Japanese paper balloon bomb. Pastor Archie Mitchell who was nearby was called for but before he could reach the scene one of the boys touched the hydrogen filled balloon bomb and it went off killing the pastor's wife Elsie (Winters) Mitchell, formally of Port Angeles, along with five Sunday School Students ranging in ages 11 to 14. Mrs. Mitchell is buried at the Ocean View Cemetery in Port Angeles. A monument stands today at the scene with the names of those who fell victim to the WWII bomb. Many Japanese civilians have visited the monument offering their apologies for that which took place during the war. It has been reported that these were the only casualties out of some 9,300 balloons that were launched from the Japanese main land during the war. Although balloons were designed to be launched from submarines they were never used. It was reported that some 300 of these paper balloons were found in the U.S. Some balloons were shot down by the US and the Royal Canadian Air forces. The Japanese were using the 70 foot tall and 33 foot diameter balloons as propaganda. Broadcasts announced great fires in the US and American public casualties up to 10,000 caused by the high and fast flying balloons. Most of the balloons were launched from December through March, when the jet stream over the Pacific is the strongest. The west coast was too damp for the bombs to start many fires.

Here On the Home Front

The Mitchell Monument stands at the only location where Americans were killed during World War II in the continental United States. The monument is located in the Fremont-Winema National Forest, near Bly, Oregon. Photo courtesy Weyerhaeuser Archives.

There were two P-38's Lightings and one P-61 Black Widow aircraft based at the Quileute Air Station for the purpose of intercepting these Japanese paper balloons. The Japanese believed the mission had been a total failure and in the meantime American B-29's had destroyed Japanese Hydrogen plants which were needed in the making of the balloons. The last of the balloons were launched in April, 1945. None were ever reported landing in Clallam County although one was found in Chimacum in Jefferson County.

John Leppell remembered local State and Beach Patrolman Boyd Rupp coming to a Forks School assembly and warning students about finding strange objects in the forest. "This was the aftermath of the Japanese launching of balloons with bombs which were coming to our coast in the jet stream. You were to be very cautious and if you found something you were to leave it alone and contact the State Patrol. This brought the war pretty close to home," said Johnny.

Boyd Rupp, portrait taken in 1943. Photo from the collection of the Forks Timber Museum.

Here On the Home Front

Japanese balloons were launched from off the Japan coast and floated inland on the prevailing winds with incendiary bombs.

Blackouts

Blackouts consisted of darkening the windows of homes and buildings with dark shades, paint, tar, shutters etc. This was to keep any Japanese aircraft or submarines from being able to spot a city or town by simply spotting the lights. Blackouts were also required on vehicles as headlamps were partially covered or in some cases even shut off while driving or parked. Here on the Olympic Peninsula the blackouts were enforced within 24 hours after the bombing of Pearl Harbor until early 1945.

George Wood of Port Angeles who was employed at the Washington Pulp and Paper mill which later became Crown Zellerbach remembered going to work that Monday morning after Pearl Harbor telling the boss "you know we are going to get orders to black this mill out."

"Oh! No bloody way," said his boss. Well by 10 o'clock that morning they received their orders to blackout all the windows and that would require many hours as the mill buildings in those days were constructed of many small windows.

"They were 12 X 18 inches. I remember them well as I used to have to replace them," remarked George. They painted the windows black starting with the seaward side. All the maintenance crews were working on windows but the machines were still running making paper. George worked until about 3 a.m. painting windows in the various mill buildings when the electricity was shut off at the mill and George was up on the roof of a 10 story building. He remembered looking across town and there were no lights, not one small glimmer. The town had been blacked out. How everyone had gotten the word George didn't know. He looked out and there was a big steam powered tug boat all lit up along with the tow of logs which were also brightly lit. The tug boat "Wonderer" was based in Port Angeles and made runs to Sekiu. A sitting duck, one might say, of this lone mariner if Jap Zeros had invaded here along the Straits. "I heard the cars pulling out of the mill driveway and I figured there was only one thing to do and that was to get out of there," said George. There he was up on the roof of a 10 story building with no flashlight and a metal circular stairway to descend in pitch darkness.

George did make it down and drove home to West 6th Street where he greeted his wife with a full camouflage of black paint from head to toe. Well the next day, after all the mill windows were blacked out with paint, they found that because the paint wouldn't adhere to putty that was on the side of the window casings you could still see light coming through.

"I don't know if a guy on a Japanese sub could have seen lights but you sure could from the beach," said George. So they finally bought plywood from the Pen Ply mill in Port Angeles that had just started up. "The first run of plywood that came off the mill was shipped to Crown Zellerbach and nailed over the windows for black outs and that worked fine," said George.

Dorothy Burr of Forks remembered blacking out their Bogachiel store by hanging blankets over the windows in the evening as soon as the sun went down. "So we were prepared for something to happen. We heard that 150 Japanese planes were going to invade Kalaloch. That was a rumor of course, but we took it pretty seriously at the time. My father LeRoy Smith was Air Raid Warden and mother and I were airplane observers," said Dorothy.

Helen Ulin of Forks remembered her husband Vic working down near Lake Quinault after the bombing and they would drive home to Forks on the weekends using only their parking lights. "It was kinda' scary. You didn't know if someone was going to jump out at you or what. The road to Forks was dark and winding," said Helen.

Marge Deinis of Port Angeles remembered covering their windows facing the water (Strait of Juan De Fuca) every night with cardboard which her dad had made. They also had to pull the curtains on the south side of the house facing the mountains. They also would turn their car lights off if driving towards the water. "You could use your parking lights as long as you weren't driving towards the water," said Marge.

My Uncle Larry McHone of Sequim remembered while living in Carlsborg in the early Forties seeing troops all over town. He also remembered the blackouts. Larry told this story of the blackout; "One night mom was looking after a baby for some friends while they were out to a dance when the mill whistle started to blow. That was the air raid alert, so mom remembered what to do during an air raid and placed the baby under a table for protection The problem was that the mill whistle was also the alarm in case of fire at the mill so all the mill workers jumped in their cars, turned on their headlights and went to the mill to put out the fire. Well so much for a blackout. The next day we were told that either a Japanese sub or a whale had ran into a submarine net in the Straits."

My mother Vay (McHone) Dunlap-Archibald also recalled one evening while ironing clothes at Washington Harbor just east of Sequim. A warden showed up at the door to check on a report that someone in the house was sending codes to the Japanese in the bay. The house windows were pretty well blacked out but there was a small area around the front window that was open enough for someone in the harbor to see a light and since the iron was plugged into the light cord hanging from the ceiling the light would swing back and forth every time the iron was in motion creating what was thought by others to be some kind of a code. The problem was soon solved and the ironing was completed. One might say it was somewhat of a pressing event here in the harbor.

Vay and Nig Dunlap's cabin at Washington Harbor.
Photo by Vay Archibald.

Bub Elvrum told of the roads not being blacktopped so you had no lines to follow after dark. "I know one time we came into Port Angeles from Neah Bay along Highway 112 and the road was gravel. We stayed after dark and it took over three hours to make it back to Neah Bay. Just try it sometime on a gravel road with your parking lights taped and pretty soon you see things that aren't there. We would stop and let our eyes rest for a while then proceed. If you drove 15 to 20 miles per hour you were doing great. You were taking a chance at 20. Your vehicle lights back in the 40's weren't that great anyway. Not like they are today. We got caught in town once and that was the last time we stayed where we would have to drive home in the dark. That was a thrill I'll tell you. It looked like the road would take off a certain way and someone would say No! No! No! No!" said Bub.

"They discouraged people from driving at night but if you had to be out at night your headlights had to be tapped. They used this old black tape with only a slit showing of the headlights. Made for some very slow driving," said Lawrence Gaydeski of Forks.

"We had what they called a Block Watch and I had an area in which to go around and see that there were no lights shining anyplace," said Maynard Lucken who was living at Lake Pleasant. Maynard also mentioned that you were supposed to keep two buckets of sand in the house in case of a fire. If you had an attic you were supposed to have a step ladder in order to get up there also in case of a fire, and you also were supposed to keep a bucket of sand in your attic.

It has been said that thousands of people died in road accidents during the blackouts. Dimmed street and car lights lead to these accidents. Also many were injured from tripping and falling from steps.

Ron Shearer remembered, in Forks, his dad using tar paper to black out the windows. "Forks never had the street lights on during the blackouts. We had a diesel operated light plant in Forks during that time. We didn't have PUD lines in the city of Forks and so people were pretty conservative of their lighting. No neon lights or anything like that. We had plenty of lighting for our homes from the old power plant, however. But it was just in town. If you lived anywhere on the outskirts of town you used gas lights," said Ron.

Eleanor (Maxfield) Thornton of Forks remembered during the war her husband Floyd as a saw filer who also ran trap lines here in the wilderness of the West End. On drives to Queets he would stop at the military camp at Ruby Beach to check in then drive on to Queets and other areas south to attend his trap lines. Driving at night on the then graveled highway, he would have to drive with either no lights at all or partial lighting which made it tough traveling on those winding roads shaded from the moonlight by tall old growth forests.

During the blackouts in some areas of the country white stripes were painted on street light poles and roads to help drivers whose car lights were dimmed. Men were asked while walking to leave their shirt-tails hanging out so they could be seen more easily by drivers.

Beverly Porter of Joyce mentioned that war brought an end to all night time activities at Crescent School. The gym and stage were located in the center of the school on the first floor. The second floor high school classrooms on the north were surrounded by a "U" shaped balcony lit by windows on the east and west. Also there were skylights over the gym. It was not feasible to blackout that much glass. Since there were no other large buildings in Joyce all activities had to be conducted during daylight hours such as basketball games, graduation etc.

Here On the Home Front

Rations

After the bombing of Pearl Harbor and the entrance into the war by the United States, consumers immediately found themselves sacrificing goods for military production for the war effort. By May of 1942 the U.S. Office of Price Administration froze prices on most everyday goods and consumers were now using ration books for buying certain items such as food. There were various reasons why certain foods were rationed. Ships, for example, which normally carried coffee and coffee beans from areas of South America were detoured for military purposes. Gas rations were also imposed to save petroleum for the synthesizing of rubber. The Japanese had seized rubber plantations in the Dutch East Indies that produced about 90 percent of the raw rubber used here in the Americas. Products made of rubber such as old tires, bathing caps, hoses, rubber shoes, etc. were being recycled. Women often substituted nylon stockings with cotton or rayon stockings. (We will discuss bottled stockings later). Shoes were also rationed as soldiers needed millions of combat boots. And the list goes on with sugar, coffee, clothing liquor, cigarettes, etc. And so it was, shoppers carried coupon books to the local stores to purchase what items they could with what coupons they had in their ration books. Stamps were colored such as blue for canned foods, red for meat, butter, cheese etc. For gasoline the average citizen would be allowed 2 to 5 gallons a week with the black "A" sticker. The amount of fuel allowed varied from one region to another and was revised at times. Stickers were placed on the windshields of the vehicles. The green "B" sticker would allow a varied amount of gas depending on your driving distance to work. The red "C" sticker was assigned to emergency vehicles and was good for whatever amount of fuel was needed to operate fire equipment, ambulances, and police vehicles as well as for doctors, mail carriers, ministers, railroad workers etc. Farmers also received an almost unlimited amount of fuel. Victory speed limits of 26 to 35 miles per hour along with car pools were encouraged. This was to save on rubber rather than fuel. This system of rationing was a pain from the consumer to the retailer to the wholesaler to the manufacture to the administrators. With rationing, however, supply and demand was controlled as was public anger. The poor could obtain needed commodities as well as the rich. There was black marketing, however. It was here in the black market that some would buy rationed items illegally at a higher price. Gasoline and sugar were just two of the items popular to profiteers.

But then it was said that the system did its job of controlling inflation and the distribution of scarce goods. Black marketing was brought about by organized crime and the counterfeiting of ration stamps. Most rationing ended by August 1945. Sugar rationing lasted until 1947 in some parts of the country with yet other items lasting even longer.

Dorothy Cline of Forks remembered having to sign up for ration books for purchase of ration stamps. "Everyone was issued their own book of ration stamps. We had to stand in line quite often," said Dorothy.

George Wood of Port Angeles also remembered that you couldn't purchase a new car during a portion of the war years.

"They had stopped manufacturing private automobiles right after the war started. You couldn't buy new cars until the war was over," said George. Because car manufacturers were then building vehicles for military use it was hard to get spare parts for private cars as well. New car production was banned January 1, 1942. Military vehicles werc being made.

John Nelson remembered when he returned from war, civilians were still on rations. Sugar, butter and meat were still hard to come by in local stores. John was use to beef in the Army and all he could find when returning home was mutton.

Betty (Ryser) Dunlap and her sister June (Ryser) Matriotti mentioned how they had a hard time buying cigarettes during the war but they could get their hands on tobacco so they rolled their own. Besides it was cheaper to roll them. June remembered they used a small wooden machine to roll their prize cigarettes. The sisters also remembered their dad making wine so he didn't miss the absence of whisky. It was hard obtaining whisky with the exception of "Old Spud" which was made from potatoes and tasted awful. They also mentioned the fact that while growing up as teenagers they had just came out of the "Great Depression" then came the war. Also Betty mentioned that there was no Sequim High School Annual in 1942 when she graduated. Living in the country and on farms they perhaps had it easier as far as having food. Chickens, beef, milk, eggs, vegetables, berries, potatoes and fruit helped them get through the "Great Depression" and also the war.

John Leppell remembered a man named Charlie McCarthy

who owned the Richfield Station in Forks during the war. The station was located at the junction of Forks Avenue and Bogachiel Way where the Olympic Sporting Goods store stands today in the Almar Building.

"When the government started gas rationing almost anybody who moved around a little bit didn't have enough gas to get out of town. There was such a thing as black market but Charlie usually had gas there and he didn't charge Black Market prices," said John. When the rationing was taking place the government would have someone come to John's father's farm to see how many tractors, pickups, hay trucks and other business vehicles he had and how many trips he would make to town and how much the equipment would be used on the farm. From this John's father was issued his gas stamps. "We had two tractors and one was hardly ever used. Then we had two hay trucks which only ran during the hay and oat season but we were given credit for operating those vehicles the year around so we were getting more gas than we really needed. When Charlie delivered gas to our farm dad would give him extra stamps he didn't need and Charlie would then pass them on to his customers at the station who were in need of the precious fuel. And so it was kind of like robbing from the rich and giving to the poor," said John

War ration book issued to Art Munson, Jr. of Beaver. From the collection of Greg Munson.

Darrel (Bub) Elvrum spoke of rations at their Neah Bay restaurant during the war. "We got help from the Navy, USCG and Army. They vouched that the restaurant was feeding troops. Meat, sugar and coffee almost tripled of what the restaurant would have received had it not been for government help. The military had asked why the restaurant never stayed open later and it was because we ran out of food. It wasn't long before some of the officers went to the restaurant and talked to Bub's mom and said they would see that the restaurant got more food supplies since they were feeding the troops. At times the Navy personnel would come ashore and eat at the restaurant just to get off the ship. The Navy wanted to throw a party so they asked Bub's mom and dad if they brought their own steaks and stuff if they could cook them in the restaurant. Mom said yes, and so they did. "There was no rough housing and the party was very orderly," said Bub. The restaurants supplies were delivered out of Port Angeles and delivery persons would comment on how much food and beverages they were going through compared to some of the larger restaurants in Port Angeles.

Inez (Halvi) Halverson of Forks told of the war days in which she canned fruit without the use of sugar. "I canned cherries without sugar then when we opened a jar we would stir in a Saccharin tablet to sweeten it. I did the same with rhubarb," said Halvi. Ella Paul, also of Forks, mentioned using honey from Mr. Graders honey bee hives for sweetener.

My mother Vay (McHone) Dunlap-Archibald told about not being able to buy nylon stockings during the war so women used leg paint, also known as bottled or liquid stockings. "We couldn't get stockings so we painted our legs. We could get different colors and if you painted the seam crooked you would have to wash it all off and start over again. If we were going to a dance we would have to start early to get ready and get our legs painted," said mother.

Viola Holman remembered churning their own butter while living in Carlsborg. For many farmers there was no cause for worry about getting enough ration stamps for dairy products when you had all the ingredients on your or your neighbor's farm. For big city folks this could be a problem.

Lawrence Gaydeski of Forks told of loggers not showing up for work because they had no boots to wear. "One of the stories I was going to tell you was you were allowed one set of shoes a year or something like that. Well some of those loggers, Hell I remember when I was working in the woods and a young man who was active on his feet a lot would wear out two sets of calk boats a year. Well these guys didn't have boats so they wouldn't show up for work. Production started falling off and there were soon questions about it and before it was all over the logging outfits were given extra stamps to give to their employees so they could buy calk boots," said Lawrence.

Pearl and Maynard Lucken of Tyee also mentioned the lack of whiskey and the horrible taste of "Old Spud" whiskey which was made out of potatoes.

Maynard thought you were only allowed a fifth of good whiskey per month. "We could buy this phony stuff back then, Marimba rum which would kill a dog, but we drank a lot of Coca Cola with it," said Maynard.

Pearl thought it was good stuff. "We saved up our liquor and when the war was over we partied," said Pearl. They also remembered the top hit song "Rum & Coca Cola" by the Andrews Sisters in 1945. It was banned by some radio stations, however, as it mentioned an alcoholic beverage.

Ella Paul of Forks remembered when her first husband Clarence Brager and she, while living ten miles south of Forks at the Huling's Mill area, used their new car as a crew bus as they were transporting loggers down to Lake Quinault to work. This along with fueling their trucks allowed them plenty of fuel.

Jackie (Kelm) Simmons of Forks mentioned her family moving from Port Ludlow to Forks in July of 1942, mainly due to gas rationing. "I think when we moved here it was probably because of gas and tire rationing because my dad Arthur Kelm had been commuting from Port Ludlow to Forks to work. He was working for Bloedel which later became Rayonier Timber Company. We would camp at Sappho during the week then drive home for the weekend. The gas and tire rationing kept people pretty close to home," remembered Jackie.

According to Jackie chocolate bars were also hard to find during the war. Jackie remembered one time when she was attending Forks High school the boys had a basketball tournament in Port Townsend and Mr. Groffman who owned a clothing store in Forks rounded up enough gas and took a load of girls over to Port Townsend.

"When we got on the road, and I remember this so plain, Mr. Groffman opened the glove box and he had a chocolate bar for each one of us," said Jackie. Special chocolate bars were being made and distributed to soldiers overseas. Chocolate that wouldn't melt in the heat and that had nutritional values. It has been estimated that between 1941 and 1945, over three billion Hershey ration units were produced and distributed to soldiers around the world.

Myron and Jackie spoke of a small house located at the corner of what is now "A" street and Spartan Avenue just south of the post office where Forks middle School stands today. That was where the rationing office was.

"Ivy Price was one of those who handed out rationing and food stamps," said Myron. They also mentioned that you would sometimes stand in line and take what you could get. There was no complaining you were glad to get what you could and you conserved on what you got like gas and tires. "Of course back in them days people didn't just take off and go every weekend either. A lot of people didn't even have cars," said Jackie.

Jackie also recalled working at various cafes in Forks during the war. "Food was rationed and we only had one kind of meat, generally, and some kind of fish products or something and you know most people who came in, especially if they were traveling through, were happy to have a choice of either a meat or fish. Some would just complain but most were happy to get whatever there was available," said Jackie who was working for Alice Coyle for a dollar an hour at the Antlers, and Slim and Dell's, then Sati Rhodes, and then Louise Gaydeski at the Greasy Spoon also known as the Evergreen Cafe.

Dorothy (Smith) Burr whose parents had the Bogachiel store located about six miles south of Forks also remembered having to deal with food and gas rations as she was a teenager attending school and working at the store after school and on weekends. She remembered her dad had to go into Forks every so often to meet with the (OPA) Office of Price Administration. It was said that throughout the nation there were more than 5,000 different rationing boards that had to deal with the war time rations.

Frances Maxfield of Quillayute Prairie told of the days of rations and some advantages they had. "We had it pretty good as my folks had their cows and milk and they churned butter. Well we made off pretty good because at that time we weren't drinking coffee or tea and they did, so we traded them our coffee stamps for butter you see. So that's the way a lot of them did," said Frances.

Frances also talked about rations on silk stockings and how they would use the leg makeup (bottled stockings) which was fine until you got the leg wet then the colored dye would streak and what a mess it was. At times they could find real stockings and many learned how to sew up the runs in these prized wares. "If you got a run or a hole in the stockings you sewed it up, you didn't throw it away," said Frances.

Betty (Pedersen) Bernier of Forks remembered while during the war living with her family of 5 boys and 4 girls in Rayonier housing in Beaver behind where the Lake Pleasant Grocery and the Beaver Fire hall and Post Office sit today. At the time they called it Tyee. Confused? Aren't we all? Sappho, what's left of it that is, sits at the junction of highway 101 and 113. Highway 113 is also known as Burnt Mountain Road leading north to Clallam Bay.

Between Sappho and Beaver (formerly known as Tyee) is Old Beaver along Highway 101 where there was once a cafe, roller rink, dance hall and tavern just south of the Beaver School. East Lake Pleasant Road runs north of Highway 101 near this location. It's called East Lake Pleasant as it runs just east of the lake but runs in a northerly direction. And then farther southwest of Old Beaver is what today we call Beaver, Lake Pleasant or by some, Tyee. Your choice, I guess.

Here West Lake Pleasant road runs north of Highway 101 along Lake Pleasant. Before we become anymore confused we will get back to what it was Betty was telling us about the war years at Tyee. Tyee? Anyway, living in a small cabin during the war (rent was $6 to $9 per month) she remembered her mother Ada using rations to buy flour. The flour sacks were saved to make the girls dresses.

"The flour sacks at that time had colored flower designs in pinks, blues, greens and were the size of gunny sacks," said Betty. Betty and her sisters wore the dresses to school at the old Beaver Grade School.

Many mothers remembered the flour and seed sacks of the Great Depression days of the 1930's. This form of clothing was continued into the war years. These 50 to 100 pound bags made of cotton became even more popular for the making of dresses when they were manufactured in checked, plaids and flowered materials. Curtains and dish towels were also made of the cotton flour sacks. During the depression families couldn't afford clothing and during the war there was little available.

Here On the Home Front

Ron Shearer, whose dad had the Shell station and distributorship in Forks, remembered gas for a while being brought into La Push by barge.

"They would bring gas into La Push by barge and right at the bottom of the hill of the old USCG station near Butts and Paterson's restaurant were some tanks. They would pump the fuel from the barge up to the tanks. We would have to go down and load up our fuel for the station and the distributorship," said Ron.

Ron also remembered a Union 76 plant at Mora at Taylor's where the barge would take fuel up the Quillayute River to the Dickey at high tide. Ron also remembered a "T" stamp for the rationing for truck fuel.

Ron also spoke of butter and margarine during the war. Butter was hard to come by so they had a substitute product called Margarine (also known as Oleo)

Rationing Calendar

PROCESSED FOODS
Blue Stamps in War Ration Book 2, R-S-T, valid now through Sept. 20. U-V-W valid now thru October 20th.

MEATS AND FATS OILS AND RATIONED DAIRY PRODUCTS
Red Stamps in War Ration Book 2—X-Y, valid now through October 2.
Brown Stamps in War Ration Book 3—A valid Sept. 12 through Oct. 2. B valid Sept. 19 through October 2.

SUGAR
Stamp 14 in War Ration Book 1, valid now through October 31.
Stamps 15-16 for home canning valid now through Oct. 31.

SHOES
Book No. 1, Stamp No. 18 valid through October 31.

GASOLINE
Coupon 7, A-Book, valid now through Sept. 21.

TIRE INSPECTIONS
A-Cars deadline Sept. 30. B-Cars deadline October 31. C-Cars deadline Nov. 30.

FUEL OIL
Fuel oil coupon No. 5 expires on September 30.
File renewal applications at once with local war price and rationing boards.

Rationing calendars and instructions published in the newspapers. From Jean Miller Collection.

which was as white as your socks, providing you were wearing white sox that is. Farmers soon lobbied as they didn't want the public to buy margarine. They wanted everyone to buy butter. The farmers demanded that margarine remained white so you could tell it from butter. To make the margarine yellow you had this little pill the size of a marble and you would puncture it with a knife and mix the dye with the margarine in a bowl.

"This was all political," said Ron. Margarine wasn't anything new, however, as you can go back to the Oleomargarine Act of 1886 when dairy interest groups pushed congress to pass the 1886 act which placed a two-cent per pound tax on margarine as well as requiring a license to sell the stuff. By 1902 more than half the states had banned the coloring of Margarine which made it look like yellow butter. For those states allowing for colored Margarine congress raised the tax to 10 cents per pound. In 1951 the federal Margarine tax system came to an end.

Ron also spoke of the old Forks liquor store which was located in Ray Ross's Olympic Pharmacy during the war. The drug store later became the Fern Gallery and then the Twilight store which on October 29, 2012 burned down along with the IOOF Hall.

Here On the Home Front

The IOOF (left) and Dazzled by Twilight building that was once the Olympic Pharmacy with a soda fountain and later the Fern Gallery, burned on October 29, 2012. Photo by Lonnie Archibald.

"Whiskey, along with other liquors was rationed. I think you were allowed a fifth a week or something like that. Oh it was just heartbreaking as these loggers a few times would come in there with their boots on the marbled floors and their feet would go out from under them and they would fall breaking their bottles. That was all the booze for that week and the weekend was shot," said Ron who at that time was too young to partake of those deviled spirits anyway. By 1944 most whiskey had disappeared from the liquor store shelves. Distillers converted over to the production of industrial alcohol.

Eunice Jones of Forks remembered operating the Joyce

General store during the war. Rations were a big thing at that time and she remembered one incident involving her son Dean. Customers at that time would make the rounds to friends and stores trying to get butter that was rationed.

We were trying to keep butter for our regular customers and I had told someone we didn't have any, we were out and Dean was just a little fellow and he said, "uuh huh, mommy we have butter," and he ran to the refrigerator to prove it and so that was kind of an embarrassing time for me," said Eunice. Eunice was also post master as the post office was in the store.

Her husband Alton spent most of his time with the store while she attended the post office. Once the mail was sorted and in the boxes Eunice would help at the store. There was quite a bunch of outgoing mail as many had friends and relatives in the service at that time.

Jack Olson of Forks after moving to Port Angeles during the war told of coming back out to Mora to stay in his folks' cabin and visit his buddies. His dad Jack had lost his home when it was taken over by the Olympic National Park in 1938, devastating his dad. His dad did have a lease on the place however. Jack remembered having an "A" stamp on his model A Ford. "I wasn't working out at Quillayute at that time so I was only allowed three gallons a week. And that Model A took about three gallons to start it, you know. I had to place the "A" stamp on the windshield. Anyway there were these Navy aviators standing in a cabin down at James's old place at Mora as they and their families would stay there. I would go down to the

Here On the Home Front

Quillayute River, catch fish and give it to those guys and in return they would bring me aviation gas and that Model A would run good on that but you had to mix oil with it or it would burn the valves out and when you shut it off it would run for about five minutes and the manifold would be red hot you know," said Jack.

To stay ahead of the meat rationing, Joe Blomgren of Forks mentioned families buying beef from local farmers during the war. In Forks old Charlie Lewis, Blonde Streeter and others were raising cattle. It was very common in those days to buy a quarter or half a steer. You would get a local butcher to cut and wrap it and put it in a storage locker. Rationing wasn't severe at all.

"You never ran out of anything. It wasn't like other countries where people were starving to death. There was always enough to go around," said Joe. "We had our ration stamps but I don't remember ever being deprived at all," said Joe's wife Virginia.

June Bowlby of Clallam Bay remembered they were gifted a big barrel of what she thinks was corn syrup and sugar was hard to get during that period of the sugar rations. "My mother used that syrup as a replacement during the war making it last quite a while," said June.

John Jarvis of Agnew spoke of gas rations; "My step-grandpa still had the farm during the war and along with dad working at the Rayonier Mill we didn't have gas to spare but we had gas to get by. We had to make a trip to Seattle for some reason, don't know why but in order to make that trip we wanted to get as much gas in the car's tank as possible. I remember we drained gas out of two model "T" Fords and we even emptied white gas out of our blow torches. We mixed all that gas together, dumped it into our Chevrolet and made the trip to Seattle and back."

Larry McHone made the comment, "we managed to get by during the war but sugar rationing sure cut into the cookie and fudge production."

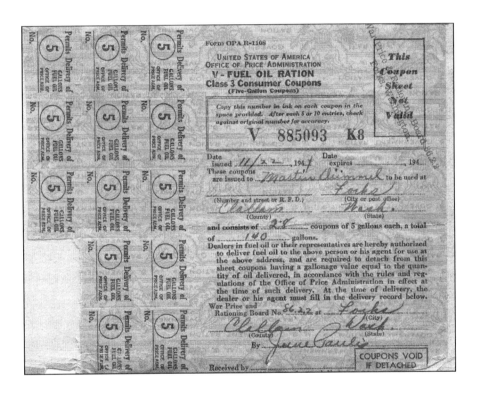

This is an example of fuel oil rationing coupons as issued to control the consumer consumption of scarce resources.
From the collection of Jean Miller.

Beverly Porter of Joyce also mentioned a shortage of film and photography materials during the war. Cameras were also hard to get. "I had class photos for every year of my schooling except for my junior and senior year. Photographers didn't come those years," said Beverly.

Shoes were another subject brought up by Beverly. "We had cardboard-soled shoes that would disintegrate if wet. You could buy them at the Family Shoe Store. The ad said "No ration stamps needed," but don't get them wet," said Beverly. The ones she wore were black fabric called "Baby Dolls". They had rounded toes and a little strap. When she went off to college at Western the students were wearing wooden shoes in which the upper portions were leather. Her parents told her that buying them was not sensible so she had to save her ration coupons and get regular saddle oxfords.

Airplane Spotters

Harvey Green who graduated from Forks High School in 1948 then went on to the University of Washington compiled the following information pertaining to the Civilian Aircraft Warning Service.

Following the December 7, 1941 Japanese attack on Pearl Harbor, Hawaii, Americans had a strong desire for revenge. The following day President Franklin Roosevelt declared war on Japan and the United States was plunged into the Second World War. A genuine fear of air raids or hostile action similar to that of Pearl Harbor was a real threat to those living here on the Olympic Peninsula as well as the country in whole. Military and civil authorities swung into action to mobilize the nation's defense.

As early as 1942, a vast network of Civil Defense organizations was set up. With the seemingly emanate threat of Japanese aircraft attacks on the mainland the Aircraft Warning Service was set up and Aircraft Spotter Shacks soon dotted the landscape. The buildings were usually raised structures, located on high ground, or in an open area where most of the sky was visible in all points of the compass. Although their sizes varied, the usual building was a square structure, approximately 15X15 feet, with windows on all four sides. Manned by volunteers from the surrounding area, they spotted aircraft, attempted to identify such features as how many engines, wings, altitude, direction of flight, and an educated guess as to which aircraft it may be. The shifts as spotters were often a family event, sometimes including three generations. Although the duty of "Aircraft Spotter" was often a family outing, it was also taken dead serious.

Pearl Lucken displays the armband that she wore, designating her as a official aircraft observer. Photo by Lonnie Archibald.

Also Filter Board Operations were set up where residents would plot aircraft sightings such as the one at the Port Angeles armory. Planes were tracked across the county then called in to Seattle. Many sightings were made, however not one single spotter had seen an "enemy aircraft."

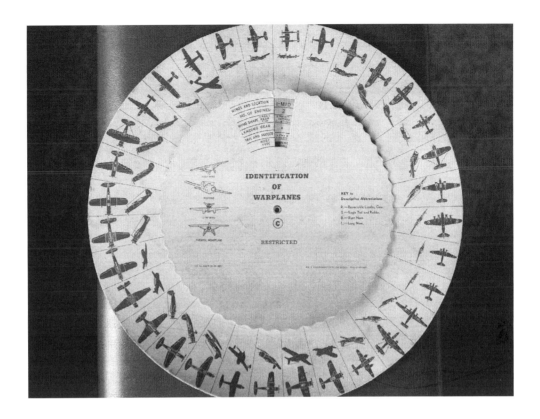

Aircraft identification disk showing silhouette configurations of airplanes. Greg Munson collection.

The spotter shacks were equipped with a telephone, maps of the general area, field glasses, compass, several large "Aircraft Identification Disks," and an "Aircraft Spotters' Handbook." The ID disks were constructed of durable white cardboard with a window that was rotated to the desired location which displayed a black silhouette view of the spotted aircraft. In addition to the ID disks, a large "Aeronautics Aircraft Spotters' Handbook" was used as a general reference. The book had an edge page index with twelve sections, indicating the number of engines, and wing position (high, mid-wing and low wing). This handbook was periodically upgraded and went through four editions during the war. Within its covers there were 350 military aircraft silhouettes, with photograph of the plane at the top of the page. The general instructions for calling in a sighting were also posted inside the spotter shack with a graphic seven step illustration.

This information was also on the inside of the Spotters Handbook and read:

"Army Flash"

When an observer sights a group of hostile planes, he picks up his telephone and says "ARMY FLASH." The Central Operator at once connects him with the assigned Filter Center to which he reports the type of planes, number, height, and direction of flight. When several reports agree, watchers transmit the data to an information center where developments over a large area are plotted on a huge map. Watching the map, Air Corps officers order interceptor planes into the air, direct them to contact with the enemy, another officer notes the cities threatened and flashes a yellow, blue, or red alarm, according to the degree of danger, to the proper Warning District Center.

Aircraft spotting towers were constructed to provide shelter and visibility for the spotters. Photo by Lonnie Archibald.

At this point, Civilian Defense takes over from the Air Corps, telephones and warning to the Control Center within the Warning District. And here the Commander of the local Citizen's Defense Corps orders the alert, has the public warning sounded

Here On the Home Front

usually short blasts on air horns, power horns or steam whistles or on the wailing sirens and if the bombers arrive overhead, directs the operations of defense.

Both Harvey Green and his wife Ione had some experiences with the spotter shack in Sappho as did Ione's parents Bruno and Myrtle Sarnowski. The shack was located near where the Bonneville Sub-station is today at the east end of Sappho.

Pearl Lucken of Beaver was also an observer at Sappho. "We had to learn the different planes, their sounds and directions of travel when we called in. Everything was dark and scary," remarked Pearl. She still has her arm band which reads U.S. Army AWS Air Force Observer. She also has pins received for her volunteering efforts during the war. Pearl also remembered Ivy Price being active in plane spotting and rationing.

Lawrence Gaydeski of Forks noted that communications during those days was very primitive to what it is today and it was all party lines.

"So when you saw or heard a plane you picked up the phone and said ARMY FLASH and if there was anyone else on the line they were to hang up immediately. If not then there would be someone knocking on their door before long," said Gaydeski. Someone like the Air Defense Warden.

Marge Deinis and June Nelson remembered Lillian (Lander) Keller who was a plane spotter on Pyramid Peak on Lake Crescent. There was a small plane spotters shack perched there on the top with a tiny walkway all the way around the building.

The girls pooled their gas rations and drove out to Sugarloaf Mountain. With sleeping bags and food they hiked the three and a half miles straight up the mountain to spend the night with Lillian. When bed time came, Lillian told her visitors that no one was allowed to spend the night inside the spotters shack and they would have to sleep outside. Lillian said she couldn't have anyone in there at night when she gave her call signals and reported any planes flying over. "These were the government rules handed to Lillian and she had to stick to her guns" replied June. And what a night it must have been sleeping on a narrow walkway high above the moon lit waters of Lake Crescent.

My Mother Vay (McHone) Dunlap-Archibald recalled my grandmother Eva (Bodenhaufer) McHone-Taylor as an airplane spotter down at the old Cook Farm where she volunteered at night. It was located near the junction of the Kitchen-Dick road and the old Olympic Highway north west of Carlsborg near Agnew.

Dorothy (Smith) Burr of Forks also held onto a collection of memorabilia. "My father LeRoy Smith had been an air raid warden and mother and I were both plane spotter volunteers so we received pins while the war was still on. When asked how she received the pins Dorothy replied, "I was about 15 and they had a program at the Olympic Theater in Forks where they gave out the awards."

Pat Mansfield of Forks remembered her mother making her go with her to the plane spotter's tower at Sappho as her mother worked there at night and was afraid of the coyotes. "I would

Here On the Home Front

look at all the silhouettes on the wall of German, Japanese and American planes. We never did hear a plane while there at the spotters shack," said Pat.

Doug McInnes of Sequim wrote in his book a story about airplane spotting. Doug's book "*Sequim Yesterday, Local History through the Eyes of Sequim Old-Timers*" was published in 2005. His remembrance went something like this. Life in Sequim changed fast after the December 7, 1941 Japanese attack on Pearl Harbor. Sequim sailors Henry Echternkamp and Marlyn Nelson, brothers of two of my sixth-grade classmates, were immediate casualties.

Officials feared invasion and soldiers arrived in Sequim the next day and were soon patrolling the beaches, stringing barbed wire and sand-bagging machine gun nests. Piles of brush burning at night near where Costco is now located were briefly suspected of being signal fires directing Japanese bombers to Boeing. (One might note that Costco at the time of Doug's writings was located at the junction of Highway 101 and Hooker Road south of Carlsborg.) Old-timers would remember it as Goven's Field. Costco has since moved to Sequim.

One wartime activity nearly forgotten now was the attempt to detect enemy aircraft before they got to inland targets. Volunteers manned many observation posts on the Peninsula. One local aircraft spotter phoned in and franticly reported a submarine going overhead. This later proved to be a dirigible.

There were full-time observers assigned to the more remote

areas. In late 1942 my brother, Rex Jr. "Bud" and his wife Jean and their baby Judy were on an observation post about 15 miles beyond Forks near the Hoh River, very close to where Allen Logging is today. One observer (listener is a more accurate description) had to be awake and listening at all times. If aircraft were heard one of them immediately phoned headquarters, identifying their post (Baker 66) and reported what they could about height, number and direction.

In the summer of '43, at age 14, I visited them for a couple weeks. They lived in a three-room cabin and carried their water uphill for a quarter of a mile.

Bud rigged a harness so his dog, Jinx, could carry his own water. They also collected rainwater off the roof. Bud learned to cook and bake while living there, specializing in pies.

The night before the pack trip we had dinner with the Fetcher family near Forks and we were served bear meat which we had never eaten before. Charlie Lewis was our packer. His wife, Marie, was the daughter of John Huelsdonk, the legendary Iron Man of The Hoh.

The pack trip to Owl Mountain was 15 miles. There were the three of us, Charlie, a radio repair man, three forest service guys about 16 years old, pack horses and riding horses. Then we left the river and the second half was a steeper climb on foot.

The cabin, perched atop Owl Mountain, had big glass windows and may have been used for spotting forest fires prior to the war. We carried water there too, even farther, and soon found that it was easier to wash clothes at the spring than carry the water. An old entry in the cabin logbook said, "June morning greets us with one inch of snow." That seemed pretty dramatic to Bud and me, having lived many years at an elevation of 10 feet - even less on a high tide. (Doug was speaking here about where he lived near the beach at Jamestown.) There was a big stump next to the cabin that had a shake roof built over it, a place to sit and listen and escape the confines of a small cabin. There was also a very large meadow on a lower hillside. To us farm boys it was strange to be way up in the mountains, far from any sign of man, and see a beautiful, never to be cut hayfield.

It is interesting to look back 60 years at those war years and realize what remarkable times they were. America went from stagnating Depression to all-out war effort in just two years. The whole network of people involved as both part-time volunteers and full-time aircraft observers was just one example of the many war efforts America undertook in World War II, the major event of the century. Again these writings were taken from Doug McInnes's book, "Sequim Yesterday."

It wasn't only adults that volunteered as plane spotters. Forks sixth grader Larry Palmer and high school students Chuck and Phil Palmer also put in many summer hours at the old plane spotters tower which was located near what is now the junction of Maple Ave and E. Division St. in Forks. They would begin in the early morning and stay until their relief came around 10A.M. Fortunately no Japanese planes had to be reported by those youngsters.

War Bonds

"It was the one time, at least in my lifetime; you didn't hear much political arguing because the whole effort was to win the war, kids and everybody. There was a program in school where they had these stamp books and kids would buy ten or twenty five cent stamps. When the book was full you could get a $25 War Bond. You had $18.75 worth of stamps and in ten years it was worth the $25. All the kids in Forks were doing that," said Lawrence Gaydeski. The name "Defense Bond" of 1940 was changed to "War Bond" after the bombing of Pearl Harbor on December 7, 1941. It was said that more than a billion dollars' worth of advertising was donated during the first three years of the National Defense Saving Program. Over the course of the war 85 million Americans purchased bonds totaling approximately $185.7 billion according to the Wikipedia encyclopedia. Besides artists, movie stars, musicians, etc, the Girl and Boy Scout Clubs of America also contributed under the slogan "Every Scout to Save a Soldier."

June Bowlby of Clallam Bay also remembered buying stamps at school every week. "Everybody was really faithful about buying them as anyone with money would, and also we had a "War Bond night" at the school auditorium where locals would make pledges to purchase bonds for the war effort. It was a big event in the community," said June.

Here On the Home Front

Available Bonds	At maturity
$18.50	$25.00
$37.50	$50
$75	$100
$375	$500
$750	$1000

John Jarvis remembered while attending school in Sequim he along with other students were invited to ride around the old tennis court holding on for dear life while the jeep often went up on two wheels.

Bert Fletcher remembered while attending school in Forks how after purchasing a certain amount of war bonds a soldier would bring a new jeep to school that had been purchased with the help of children purchasing the bonds. "They actually brought two jeeps and the soldier who was staying with my grandparents was one of the drivers. And so we would pile on, and this was a safety man's nightmare as there must have been twenty of us kids hanging all over these jeeps as they would drive us around town. It was a big thrill," said Bert.

Bert also told of planes being bought with moneys from war bonds. "At defense plants the employees would buy bombers or fighters.

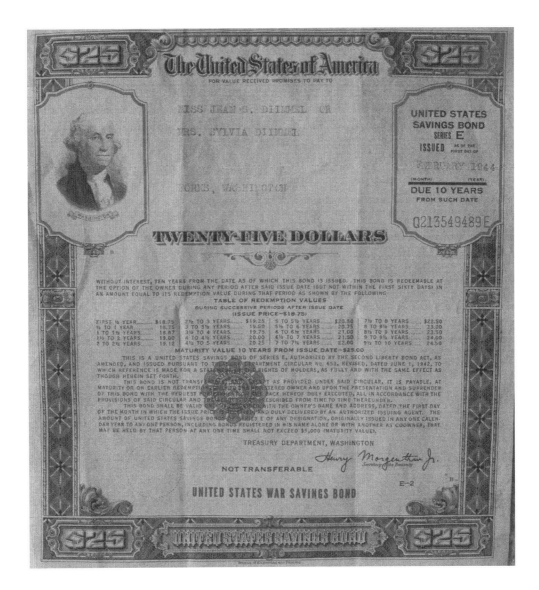

War bonds were issued in a variety of denominations. Bond from Jean Miller collection.

Let's say they were building bombers at a certain plant. Well they would have a bond drive where you buy savings bonds and once they bought $100,000 worth or so, that would pay for a bomber.

Here On the Home Front

Then before the plane would go out they would put a message on the side of it saying that this plane was paid for by the employees of North American Aviation or Boeing or whichever company had made the plane. Then it would go straight to the military with that wording on the side." said Bert.

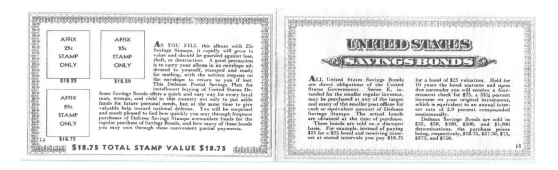

A savings album allowed installment buying of savings bonds in 25 cent increments. When the value of the stamps totaled $18.75 provided a bond with a value of $25.00 after 10 years. Savngs Bond from Judy Stipe collection.

County Quota Tremendous in Third War Loan

The people of Clallam county are face to face with a tremendous task, the purchase of $1,100,000 in United States war bonds and stamps to meet its assigned quota in the Third War Loan Drive, which begins September 9, Roy S. Jensen, chairman of the Clallam county war finance committee announced today.

In arriving at county quotas, the treasury department statisticians took into consideration many factors, prominent among which were the known income payments to citizens of the county bank deposits of all types, population per capital wealth.

The Washington state quota is $191,000,000.

Clallam county residents, meeting assigned quotas each month since the sale of bonds began, have been purchasing $105,000 and over, in war bonds monthly. The third war loan quota, to be purchased during the month of September, is ten times the normal monthly quota. The treasury department is hopeful that approximately 50 per cent of the quota in the third war loan drive will be raised by sale to individuals, the remainder being purchased by organizations, institutions and corporations.

During the second war loan drive here last spring, the assigned quota to the county was $480,150. The county oversubscribed almost $200,000, its purchases totaling $663,037.

Chairmen for the county communities are Forks, A. A. Fletcher; Clallam Bay, Hazel Murray; Neah Bay, Guy O. Coy and Sequim, Mary Brown; Port Angeles, Edward Rapp.

Newspapers included regular information about bonds, rationing, and other war efforts to encourage people to participate. Jean Miller collection.

Here On the Home Front

V-Mail

The V in V-mail stood for Victory. Ron Shearer of Forks remembered receiving V-mail from his brother who was overseas. The Servicemen would write their letters on regular sized paper. "I think it was then photographed and shrunk down on microfilm which was sent to a processing center then printed on a small sized V-Mail letter," said Ron This would save space for the postal service. Of course the letter would be censored by the government before being shipped to the home address.

Ivan and Dorothy (Smith) Burr of Forks spoke of V-Mail used while Ivan was fighting in Europe. "Whenever I wrote a letter home it would be on thin paper and censored by the government. I could pick up the stationary at the PX. Wording was often either blacked out or even cut out by the military before being sent on to family and loved ones waiting back home. I remember one time my folks had sent me a pocket book and there was an article in there about a European mountain. When I was there in Europe the mountain erupted. It lasted for ten days. When I wrote my letter home I mentioned the book they had sent me and that that was where I was at. Well they cut that part out as they didn't want anyone to know our location," said Ivan. Ivan mentioned that every day there would be a mail call and that a big sack of mail would arrive and sometimes you would receive a letter from home.

Here On the Home Front

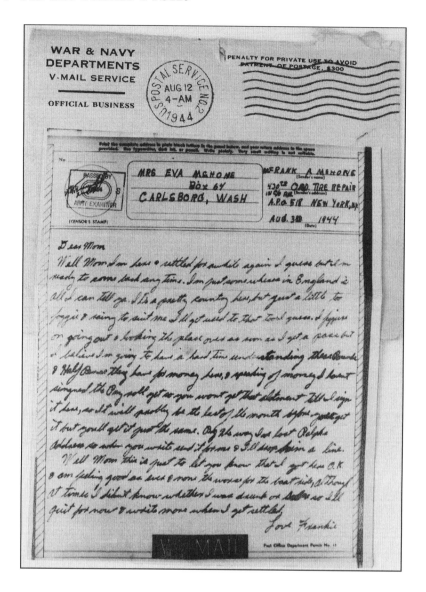

V-Mail received by Eva McHone of Carlsborg.
From the collection of Eva McHone-Taylor.

Beverly Porter while attending college at Western in Bellingham spoke of V-mails sent to her by her, then friend, Ray Porter from the South Pacific while in battle. None of those V-mails were blacked out or cut out. A good choice of wording I suppose was the reason. "Some of my girlfriends up at college however would receive V-mail that looked like confetti," said Beverly.

And of course all friends and relatives of our military heroes anxiously awaited those heartfelt letters back here in Clallam County Washington. *Here on the Home Front.*

Here On the Home Front

V-Mail Christmas greetings received by the Martin Diimmel family in Forks. From the collection of Sylvia Diimmel.

USO Club

Ron Shearer remembered the old school building located on the east side of what today is Spartan Avenue and across from Leppell's Flowers & Twilight Central store as being used for the Washington Guard until about late 42 or early 43, when the guard moved out and it became the USO Club (United Service Organizations.) This was a nonprofit organization that provided entertainment, programs and other services to our troops. It is said that nearly one and a half million Americans volunteered in the USO program during the war. There were also star entertainers such as Bob Hope, Irvin Berlin, Glen Miller and the Andrews Sisters who traveled across the nation and overseas to entertain troops and their families. "Well this little building only had a couple pool tables so mother would go and take care of that. She would sit and talk to the guys as the servicemen would come and go but there was no drinking or carousing or whatever you know," Said Ron. The building burned just a few years after the war.

In Port Angeles a USO Club was set up in the basement of the Elks Building. Virginia Blomgren of Forks also remembered going down to an encampment across the road from Ruby Beach south of Forks. "The USO wanted to gather up all the Forks girls they could and go down there for a party. There was a hall there where the soldiers and girls could dance. There were so many young soldiers, you know, that were homesick and wanted the company of girls their own age. They would pick us up in an army truck and take us down there. We would ride on benches in the back of the truck. About 20 or 30 of us. And they always

Here On the Home Front

had a chaperone from the USO. We would also go down to Ruby Beach on picnics," said Virginia. There were times they would also go to La Push to dance and visit with the Coast Guard.

The school buildings in Forks. The building in the foreground was used by the USO during the war. Photo from the Forks Timber Museum collection.

Victory Gardens

As part of the War effort the government encouraged civilians to raise fruits and vegetables. During the war it was hard to harvest and transport commercial fruits and vegetables due to a shortage of labor. Gardens soon could be found springing up in almost any location where dirt was available or could be moved to. Citizens would grow their own gardens supplying the family with fruits and vegetables. Of course the overwhelming populations of those living in the country already were growing their own peas, carrots, beets, radishes, corn, potatoes, rhubarb, apples, cherries, beans, cabbage, lettuce, strawberries, tomatoes, and more. In the cities however gardens began showing up on rooftops, local parks, baseball fields, school yards, empty lots, window boxes, and about anyplace that would prove sufficient for the growth of the much needed food.

Various magazines of that time period gave instructions on how to cook and preserve the harvested products. They also ran photos of posters with such slogans as "Your Victory Garden Counts More Than Ever," "Dig On For Victory," "Sow The Seeds of Victory," "Plant A Victory Garden, A Garden will Make Your Rations Go Further," Are You a Victory Canner?" "Save Money The Easy Way, Grow A Garden, It's Thrifty, It's Patriotic, Plant Today," "Uncle Sam Says Garden to Cut Food Costs."

Pressure cookers were purchased and canning became a household event. These gardens besides feeding local families also allowed for more supplies to be shipped overseas to our troops fighting for freedom.

Here On the Home Front

According to "*Wessels Living History*," It was estimated by The US Department of Agriculture that more than 20 million victory gardens were planted. Fruit and vegetables harvested in those home and community plots was estimated to be 9-10 million tons. This amount equaled all the commercial production of fresh vegetables. Yes the Victory Garden effort made a difference *Here on the Home Front*. A food shortage did occur in 1946, however, as many of the gardens were abandoned before commercial harvesting had reached its potential.

Lawrence Gaydeski remembered the Victory Gardens as being patriotic as citizens all pitched in growing vegetables. "Everything was focused on the war effort. They figured out some way to get people involved. That was one time this country was united in a common goal," said Lawrence. How times have changed.

Beverly Porter of Joyce told of a very large potato garden being planted at Crescent School in 1942 during the war. She remembered Bea Blore teaching there at that time and that she was quite instrumental in the planting and harvesting of the garden.

Victory Gardens were a family activity for the Diimmel family of Forks. Photo from the collection of Sylvia Diimmel.

Here On the Home Front

Victory Gardens and home canning were promoted by a poster campaign, as were many home-front efforts.

Farming, Gardening & Canning

John Leppell mentioned the effect the war had on local farmers. With the draft there were few young men around to help with farm work. Those who were available to work the farms were working long hours from the milking of cows in the early morning to driving tractor in the fields tell dark. "Come haying season there was no one around and my dad who was a heavy equipment operator worked the farm in the morning then drove cat for logging operations in the afternoon shift. The loggers in the summer were working two shifts. He was close enough to the loggers that some of those guys after working in the woods would come and help us hay at night. We would work until dark. It was pretty important on a dairy farm to have your hay," said Johnny.

"Jimmy Mansfield, Little Leo Nelson, I and Darrell Klahn would drive the hay trucks and my dad jokingly would warn the crew, "Don't anyone tell a bedtime story cause all my truck drivers will go to sleep." They were all just kids you see," said Johnny. Of course women would pitch in as well but then they also had their regular house chores you know. Darrell Klahn also mentioned how farmers, come haying season, would travel to your farm to help with the harvest then you would go to theirs to help in return.

There were always big suppers prepared by the women folk during those times. Lawrence Gaydeski remembered that meat was rationed along with a long list of hard to get goods. There on the farm in the Sol Duc Valley (spelled Soleduck back then however,) his family raised beef cattle as several others did here on the Olympic Peninsula. He remembered his dad had friends and relatives working in the shipyards in Bremerton. "They would call the old man and he would butcher a beef. Two or three of them would come over and take the beef. In those days you didn't have much in the way of freezers so they must have taken the meat home to can. I don't know what they did with it. I can remember the old man would butcher and you had to can everything. I remember my dad would come in and flop a quarter of a cow on the kitchen work table for my mother and she would be all day cutting that meat up and canning it. She had a wash boiler and then latter on got a pressure cooker," said Lawrence.

"My folks had a fruit room out back in a shed there that was attached to the house and when winter came around if mother didn't have 500 quarts of canned meat, vegetables and fruit she would panic. They even canned butter. They had a tin can sealer and would pack the butter into tin cans and seal it. They wouldn't process it or anything and it would keep and when it was needed they would open a can of butter," said Lawrence.

Lawrence also spoke of his folks preserving chicken eggs. "When the chickens were laying in the summertime my folks would take these surplus eggs, more than they could use, and place them in a five gallon crock containing a sodium and water mixture which was a slippery slimy stuff. Well the eggs would keep for several months but the only thing after they had been in there a while they weren't too good for frying as when they hit the frying pan they would just kind of splatter all out but they worked ok for baking cakes and such," said Lawrence.

"My mother also canned wild blackberries and razor clams. Like I say people survived back then. It was a different world," said Lawrence.

Walt Fuhrman who grew up on Fuhrman road south of Forks along the waters of the Bogachiel river also mentioned as other West Enders had that his family raised and grew much of their own food. "My dad had chickens, pigs, cows, and horses. We got two sheep from Tom Mansfield and mother named them Hitler and Mussolini. About the only thing we got in town was coffee and cheese. We had our own spuds and made bread and we had a root cellar. We canned chicken and everything and placed some food in crocks such as pork which would last all winter. We also had cherry and apple trees and put up our own hay. And of course we had our own milk. My mother also had bee hives so we had lots of honey."

"Our water came from a spring on the side hill and the water got to tasting bad one time so I went up and looked and there was a civet cat in the spring and half of its hide was gone," said Walt. They didn't buy water at the store back then you see. No! Not *Here on the Home Front*.

Pearl and Maynard Lucken of Tyee also remembered what you might consider as farming. "We had a cow and Maynard would be late coming home from work to milk the cow and I tried to learn but I didn't do a very good job but I learned to make my own cheese and butter and we had to do that," said Pearl. Yes they did need that here in Clallam County. *Here on the Home Front*.

Here On the Home Front

In the Sequim-Dungeness Valley, my mother remembered picking peas prior to the war. On the days she and a friend didn't have a car to drive they walked from Carlsborg to Dungeness to the pea fields. Picking peas was kind of hard as you had to carry your own hamper of peas up to have them checked out and they were heavy. You got 25 cents a hamper if you stayed the entire season. If you didn't stay you got 22 cents," said mother. The peas were shipped to Sequim to the grain elevator for processing then shipped out by train. There were lots of strawberry fields, raspberries and fruits in Sequim during those war years and for many years to come.

Frances Maxfield of Quillayute Prairie remembered most people outside of the town of Forks raised their own gardens along with cattle and chickens. When asked about how hard it was to get feed for the cattle, Francis replied, "We just fed them hay. We planted oats and cut those for hay." And then of course the cattle would graze on the pasture lands there on the Quillayute Prairie. There is an old threshing machine on display at the Forks Timber Museum that was used by several farmers in the Forks area.

Glen Price of Forks, who was living in Beaver at the time, remembered working in the hay fields for Conley in the summer. "They never paid me any money, but in the fall they butchered a beef and gave some to the folks," said Glen.

Glen also remembered his parent's old root cellar with thick walls filled with sawdust. "It would stay cool in the summer and never froze in the winter. We had a good sized garden in which I would have to hoe a row a day before I could go play. Deer and salmon were also smoked and cured in a crock of salt. It would last until the following spring then you would have to soak it in water at least all day to remove the salt," said Glen.

Glen also remembered in Beaver having a large orchard of apple and cherry trees. "Dad would sit there along the railroad track every year and shoot a bear for lard. Bear lard made good pastry as mother made bread," said Glen. "Dad was really a good hunter and he kept four or five families in deer and elk meat. He also fished the Sol Duc River and brought home buckets of trout for everybody to eat. Dad was always looking for honey trees. He had two or three hives and we would hang the honey in a pillow case and let it drip into a container. I remember one time grandma was up and the bees swarmed and we were standing back watching and they got into a ball on a raspberry bush. Grandma went out there with a box and set it down and wearing no gloves or nothing she picked those bees up and set them in the box without even getting stung. We were standing quite a ways away," said Glen. Razor clams and smelt from Steamboat Creek near Ruby Beach were also gathered and canned. Those country folks made do, you see.

Jack Olson of Forks was living part of the time on the Quillayute Prairie during the war and remembered having a cow, chickens and pigs. They too, like so many others, had access to deer, elk and fish. "Old Bill Wentworth who lived on the Little Quillayute Prairie would come down and show me how to fish. The slough there in front of the house on the Quillayute River was full of cutthroat trout. The old cat would come along with us and half the fish would go to the cat. Anyway I was going to tell you about the chickens. My cousin Don Clemons and I, when my folks went to town, found a bottle of whisky. 'Did you ever see a chicken drunk?' asked Don. 'No I never seen a chicken drunk,' replied Jack. Well these two country boys commenced to pour the distilled goods into the chicken mash."

"The chickens would sit up there on their roost and go ah, ah, ah, ah then summersault and hit the darn floor. That was the darndest thing I ever seen. When my dad came home I thought he was going to kill both of us," said Jack. I guess there was still some humor left *Here on the Home Front*. Perhaps not so humorous to the chickens however.

John Jarvis of Agnew also spoke of canning fruits and vegetables. They also preserved fish by laying layers of fish in a large crock and salting it down. "The salmon was pretty salty but I'm from a Finnish culture and one of the meals that we ate anyway was just boiled potatoes, onions, and salted fish. We would take that fish and just rinse it off a little bit, slice it real thin and eat it. Just salted salmon. Not smoked or cooked. The salt cured it. Then mother would make scalped potatoes and instead of using ham or something she would put salted fish in it. My dad gaffed the salmon down at the mouth of Siebert creek. Dad was caught by a game warden one time and he asked him what he was doing and dad said he was taking them home to feed the family and the warden just said for him not to take to many," said John. John's grandparents were also milking cows and the milk was being shipped to the Sequim-Dungeness Creamery.

WWII In Clallam County

Beverly Porter of Joyce remembered her mother hauling milk cans of cream from Joyce to Port Angeles. She would remove the back seat of the 1937 Studebaker to make way for the large cans. She also at times transported a few of the neighbors with their cream. This was quite a heavy burden on the old Studebaker with its leaf springs and oversized springs were hard to get but Beverly's father finally got hold of heavier springs and the car made its way past the bridge checkpoints in route to Port Angles with their goods.

Jim Mansfield remembered working the farm there in Forks during the war. With the help of his grandfather who died in 1944, his mother Marian, and brother Dave they kept the farm going. Art and Bob Reynolds and young Harry Reynolds also helped out on the Mansfield farm. They raised cattle and sheep, sold milk and also leased 40 acres to a Sequim company who raised peas. The peas were then taken to Sequim for shipping. Jim also spoke of delivering milk to the Forks Creamery located on Calawah Way behind what today would be the old Vagabond cafe. Jim was able to obtain a special drivers license as he was only 14 at the time. "It was an agricultural permit," said Jim. He converted his 1931 model "A" coup to a pickup by removing the rumble seat. After milking the cows each morning he would drop the milk cans off on the way to school then pick up the empties on the way home. "In them days everyone on the farm worked in order to pay the taxes, eat and survive," said Jim.

Jim also mentioned as had many others that his mom had a large garden and did a lot of canning of fruits and vegetables. We also raised and butchered sheep. They had no freezers back

Here On the Home Front

during the war so they canned meat. Jim's wife Pat mentioned also that during the war when living in Tyee with no electricity her folks had a cold box which was just a wooden cupboard in the outside wall with a screen attached to the outside so air could flow through. This of course didn't work so well during the summer in 80 degree temperatures. She also mentioned that she heard on TV recently that before refrigerators the average housewife spent 6 hours a day preparing meals. Everything had to be fresh and cooked. You didn't pull it out of the fridge or freezer and place it in the microwave as we do today. After the unfavorable use of the cold box, Pat's family upgraded to an ice box. You needed to know what it was you were after and where it was located in the ice box before you opened the door so as not to melt the ice so quickly. You didn't leave the door open long like we do today.

The ice was delivered once a week. Howard Sarnowoski who lived in Tyee remembered a man by the name of George Rowland who lived in Sappho and delivered the ice blocks in that area. Betty (Pedersen) Bernier who also lived in Tyee at that time remembered her dog biting old George one day as he entered the house with the coolant. Refrigerators and freezers more similar to what we have today were becoming more available during the 40's but of course you had to have electricity. Jim also mentioned the old diesel powered electric plant that supplied Forks during the war with the much needed electrons. "It was located where the PUD warehouse sits today and what a noise it made," said Jim. There was a large pool of water there to cool the diesel engine and Jim always thought it would be a good place to swim but there was a high fence around it that discouraged such ventures. Today the use of freezers and refrigerators has all but eliminated the use of ice boxes, crocks, and root cellars for the preserving of fruit, vegetable and meats. Things have definitely changed since the war here in Clallam County. *Here on the Home Front.*

Here On the Home Front

Industry

Bud Holman who was living in Carlsborg during the war remembered the Carlsborg Mill being down for a while prior to the war during the depression. The mill was sold in 1936. "When the war started that gave them a shot in the arm. They could sell everything they could produce. The mill ran pretty good then. A lot of lumber was shipped out on the train," said Bud. Then in 1945 the mill was closed due to a strike order from AFL.

Another memory brought back by Bud was that of the old Loki which carried logs from up at Slab Camp south of Carlsborg to the mill. The tracks ran from the mill pond up across Arvie Smith's Farm, across highway 101 then up near the junction of the Hooker and Atterberry roads. The old engine would make its way up to the camp, where loggers who lived there in bunkhouses were cutting the timber, then return to the mill around 4:30 or 5:00 each evening. Bud recalled a Mr. Hunter engineering the train. According to Bud, Hunter also operated the Carlsborg Tavern. There was also another Slab Camp rail line which ran southwest of the mill.

Maynard Lucken of Tyee, who was deferred from the military due to working in the timber industry harvesting timber from above Beaver Lake, remembered putting in ten hour days seven days a week as lumber was needed for military construction. "I remember when they built the barracks at Quillayute there wasn't a knot in the boards, it was all number one stuff," said Maynard. Maynard had earlier worked on a tug boat on Lake

Here On the Home Front

Pleasant for the Lake Pleasant Shingle Co. According to Pearl Lucken, Smiths Mill on Lake Pleasant started up in 1939 and after Pearl Harbor many women took the place of those men who went off to war.

My father Delbert "Nig" Dunlap of Carlsborg was also exempt from military service when the war broke out as he was working with military installations on Indian Island in Jefferson County.

Pete Capos of Port Angeles spoke of the local economy which relied on the mills running during the war such as Crown Zellerbach, Fiberboard, and Peninsula Plywood. "Pen Ply opened up in 1941 and of course the war came along and a lot of them were saying that if the war hadn't happened the mill might not have made it but boy they really made it," said Pete. According to Pete those who had shares in that mill would have made good money.

Glen Price who lived at Beaver during the war remembered Smiths Shingle Mill. Logs in those days were brought in by train and dumped in the lake where a tug would pull the rafts of logs to the mill sites. Logs were also trucked in and dumped farther up the lake. A lot of logging and mill activity was going on back then for the war effort. He also remembered Smith's having a power plant driven by steam. According to Merle Watson, lines were run from the mill to Smithville and on to the Lake Pleasant store. Those who were hooked up had power from 6 a.m. until about 9 p.m. while the mill was running.

Glen also remembered his dad logging for Rayonier during the war and being exempt from the draft as lumber was needed for the war effort. Bloedel-Donovan sold out to Rayonier in 1945. Glen recalled logs being shipped by train around the back side of Gunderson Mountain then back north behind Tyee Ridge to Sekiu where they were then rafted up the straits.

Everyone worked back during the war said Ernie and Joelene Wittenborn of Forks. There were jobs they couldn't even fill. Anyone who wanted to work worked. Ernie remembered the very young and the very old working in the woods, even setting choker. They didn't pay much attention to your age during the war.

Jack Olson of Forks, who was living at Mora during the beginning of the war, moved with his folks to Port Angeles in about 1942. "I drove a delivery truck when I was 14 years old for McCart's Grocery in Port Angeles located at 112 East Front Street. I had to obtain a special permit to drive at my age. I met all the dogs in town but I got along with them. Never had a dog bite me," said Jack. I can almost see that old delivery truck now as it putts its way up Cherry Street followed by excited dogs looking for a free handout of fresh market goodies.

Staples and Fancy Groceries-Fresh Fruit and Vegetables, Butter, Cheese and Eggs, Salt, Smoked Meat and Cured Meats, Flour, Feed, Seeds and Cereals, were advertised by the market. "Not many workers available during the war," Jack remembered, "many women working at the mills as well." Jack also worked at Montgomery Ward and the Fiberboard mill during the war.

Here On the Home Front

Virginia Blomgren of Forks remembered her Huling family owning a shingle mill south of Forks. "There were quite a few orders. We shipped a lot of shingles to Texas. We would truck the shingles to the rail head near Rosmond's mill near the junction of the La Push Road and Highway 101. The Port Angeles Western Railroad would then haul the shingles to Port Townsend where the railroad cars full of shingles were then barged across Puget Sound," said Virginia.

Shingles from Huling's Mill were being shipped all over during the war. The mill at that time ran on steam produced from burning its own cedar waste.

Art Anderson of Forks spoke of his car business at the beginning of the war. "I sold Studebakers, Chryslers, Terraplanes, and Packards. I had two new Plymouths sitting on the floor when they drafted me and they froze them, I couldn't sell them and they set there for a year or so," said Art. Cars were heavily rationed in 1942 until someone was found that could demonstrate significant need for a car then they were sold. Automobile manufacturing plants were building for the Armed Forces. "The cars were owned by Bart Murray over at Clallam Bay," said Art.

Beverly Porter of Joyce remembered her father Jim McNally working on a pile driver at Sekiu during the war. Jim was employed by Ozette Timber Company headquartered at Beaver but was working as a pile driver for Port Angeles Western Railroad at Sekiu. When war came, however, he was told he couldn't work on the waterfront because he had no identification. He sent back to Wisconsin for his birth certificate and all it said was "Baby Boy McNally, born July 4," 1886 but his dad had said, and his mother had told him, he was born July 4, 1887 as James Henry McNally. Well there were no family members living during the war that could verify the correct date of birth so he just took that birth certificate he had obtained from Wisconsin and got his photo ID. "We wondered and speculated did he have a baby brother who died at birth, never given a name and then the next year he was born?" said Beverly. Once back to work Beverly's mother would take Jim, along with other workers, to Sekiu each Sunday evening where they would spend the week at work returning home Friday evening. "Mother had a 1937 Studebaker and received a special gas rationing stamp allowing for more gas to transport the workers," said Beverly.

James McNally ID card issued by the U.S. Coast Guard in 1942.

Here On the Home Front

The Smith Shingle Mill on Lake Pleasant at Beaver employed many during the war years.

Logging Spruce

John Leppell mentioned the logging of Spruce here in the Forks area. There was a lot of Spruce that was logged in Forks during the war. One user of the spruce was the Patrol Torpedo (PT) boats. The reason spruce was used was that radar was just coming in and the wood wouldn't show as easily on the radar. Spruce also made for lighter and faster boats. Mahogany was also used as was plywood. Several companies made PT boats. Small and fast, some were known to have kept a float for several hours after being cut in half by enemy fire.

Some Spruce was shipped to England where they made the mosquito bombers. Some of those planes were built and then sent back to the United States. Like the PT boats, they also weren't as easily detected by radar. Nanson Anderson of Forks was one of those loggers cutting and shipping Spruce from the Hoh River. Logging was important enough that loggers would get a deferment from the draft.

Darrell Klahn mentioned they had some kids driving logging trucks such as Carter Warren and Don Britten both 15 year olds who were hauling logs out of the Hoh on Mack trucks.

Myron Simmons of Forks remembered Forks being a busy place with loads of large logs being hauled through town. Ozette Camp, Bloedel and Olympic logging were just a few companies that were going strong. "Olympic was doing some selective logging way up on the Hoh and the South Fork. All up above the Hulesdonk homestead was selective logging. There were lots of trucks with big logs going through town," said Myron.

Logs were going to reloads. Myron remembered Lloyd Kitchel, Noss Gossage and Wayne Cline running reloads. Logs were then shipped to Port Angeles by the Port Angeles Western Railroad. Back then many loggers would stay in camp and come home on the weekend. "You can't imagine some of the Timber that went through here," said Myron. "Harley Witherow, Gene & Elmer Fraker, Joe Damon, and the Chandler Brothers. All of these guys had a lot of trucks. And man they hauled some of the prettiest Spruce."

Jackie Simmon's dad Arthur Kelm logged the 6000 line up behind Lake Pleasant where they were picking up some of the logs that had been cut during WW I for the Spruce Division and then left as the war had ended before much of the Spruce Division facilities were completed.

Myron also remembered when he was in school working eight hours in the summertime for Jefferson County up on the Hoh; "Old man Undi, Brandeberry, Frank Andrys, Ells Whitehead and a lot of them guys were up there and I thought I was getting big money as I was getting $1 an hour and then they put me to work falling timber with old Bill Jardeen and I wasn't old enough and didn't have a work permit to do that job. You had to be sixteen and you had to have a work permit." Well within a week they offered Myron $9.20 a day and got him the permit to stay up there and cut timber. That was big money. They were cutting right-of-way up on the Hoh River near the Huelsdonk Ranch.

PT Boats were made almost entirely out of wood, including light and strong spruce from the Pacific Northwest forests. PT-564 underway, US Navy Photo

Here On the Home Front

Women in the Work Place

John Nelson had been working at the Rayonier mill in Port Angeles when the war broke out. John joined up for the service then returned home before going overseas and was surprised at the amount of women working at the mill. "They did men's work there," replied John's wife June. After the war in the fall of 1945, men had returned home. John believed that most women were glad to leave the mill and return to their home life and live the life they did before Pearl Harbor, although a few did stay on.

John spoke of the train rides he had taken and the women working the rails. "I was always fascinated when I was riding the train back and forth between Camp McCoy, Wisconsin and Seattle. I would see these women out there with their oil cans and grease instruments, lubricating the old engines as they came into the stations and checking various mechanical parts on the cars. A lot of them were doing men's work."

June Nelson and Marge Deinis as volunteers with the USO (United Service Organization) remembered an older lady, well at that time back in the 40's she seemed old, was going around with her little sewing machine sewing on the new stripes for those young soldiers who had earned such accomplishments. "And one time I remember we went out to Fort Hayden and all these guys were lined up and everybody had gotten a promotion or some change in rank and needed something done and we were sewing them up by hand," said Marge. The USO crew consisted of all women and Marge remembered one of the truck drivers as being Elaine Sandison. It was estimated that a few

Here On the Home Front

months after Pearl Harbor there were 80,000 women working in war plants across the nation. Scores more were soon employed in the work place.

Toni (Becker) Kettle of Sequim had gone to Long Beach California and worked as a riveter for Douglas Aircraft in 1943-44. "We all had to run to catch the busses and there were these midgets who had a hard time keeping up so some of the men would pick them up and swing them on their backs carrying them so as not to miss the bus connections. The midgets could work in small confined areas like the airplane wings," said Toni.

In Forks Jackie (Kelm) Simmons worked in the laundry room running a steam press at the Quillayute Air Base while still in high school. "I was doing officers clothes and sheets and that was fun and I learned a lot. I would catch the "Liberty Bus" in Forks and ride to the Quillayute," said Jackie. There were many Forks folks working in various capacities at the base along with military personnel living in Forks.

In Port Angeles Donna Sylvia remembered working at the Peninsula Plywood mill which had only been operating for a short time. Donna pulled plywood sheets after school and on weekends. "They were real dry sheets and not very heavy," remarked Donna. Donna thought she got about seventy five cents an hour.

Marge Cowan of Beaver applied for a job at the Quillayute Air Station after her husband Norm, who had been stationed at the USCG Base in Neah Bay, was shipped out to the South Pacific.

"I got a job right away. I set tables for civilian workers and was secretary to Mr. Jefferson Smith who was the civilian personnel director. Smith was in charge of construction of the buildings by civilian workers. They were constructing the commander and medical officer's quarters just inside the East gate on the north side of the road. They also built a medical facility. The base was a nice place to work," remarked Marge. Marge also remembered 12 Quonset huts being constructed.

"We had 24 hour a day telephone service to the base so we had to have 3 operators every day. Rita Heathers, Jean Streeter, and Mary Ann Beebe were three operators I remembered. The Telephone facilities were inside the administration building. The three would take the various shifts. They handled outside calls as well as inter Base calls. There was a big PX and Betty (Pedersen) Bernier worked there along with Zell Conley. Fred Shaw was a mechanic and Frank Andrys, Bill Long, and Joelene Wittenborn also worked there at the Base," said Marge.

Maynard Lucken, while working at the Quillayute Base, remembered Joelene Wittenborn waiting tables along with Winnie Klepps.

Frances Maxfield of Quillayute Prairie worked at Boeing on airplane wings during the war. "There were these inspectors and the planes were inspected and boy if there was something wrong with them and it was on your shift you stayed until the inspection passed. These were the B-17's," said Francis. Francis was a riveter and her husband Art was a mechanic also for Boeing. She mentioned that they had passes with a number and

Here On the Home Front

their names that were required to enter the Boeing plant.

Ron Shearer who was attending Forks Junior High at the start of the war remembered that many of the young men teachers went into the service. It was mostly women teachers during the war. He also remembered some retired teachers coming back to teach. But back then most of the teachers were women to start with.

"Well you know Marge Cowan, she was the one that got me the job out at the Quillayute Airbase for the summer. Since she knew I needed money to buy my school clothes, Marge decided to get me a job. I was only 14 and had to get a work permit. I worked at Ship Service. We had a little bit of everything there for the servicemen. Kind of like what was called a PX on Army posts and NEX on Navy posts. We even had hamburgers and ice cream cones. I use to deal out millions of ice cream cones," said Betty (Pedersen) Bernier of Forks who was living in Beaver during the war. Betty had to be careful with the ice cream. "Get rid of the cockroaches," said the servicemen. "We don't want them in the bottom of our ice cream cones." Betty would shake the metal table and strike it with an instrument to chase off the creepy critters. (See Remembering Quillayute Cockroaches by John Leppell on page 77 and Walt Fuhrman page 79.)

"Marge Cowen would pick me up and take me to Forks where we could take the Liberty Bus to the base. Marge got off work early one day and when I got off I had no ride home. Three sailors had to go to Forks so they got a jeep and took me home to Beaver. When I got home my dad said "What the Hell is going on." "Well! I missed the bus. The sailors were laughing and dad was pretty nice about it then," Said Betty.

Beverly Porter of Joyce spoke of her situation after high school beginning college at Western Washington College in Bellingham in 1943. "I was doing my student teaching my senior year with only two requirements left to finish college and they offered us 'War Emergency Certificates' as they were so short of teachers. So I took the certificate and went to Davenport, Washington making $2,000 a year teaching fourth grade. They were only paying $1,895 at that time in Everett," said Beverly. After earning more credits at Eastern Washington College in Cheney and teaching at several other schools after the war she ended up years later back home teaching at Dry Creek west of Port Angeles.

Jim Mansfield of Forks mentioned his father Tom was post master prior to the war and then his mother Marian took over as temporary post master when Tom went into the service working at both the Quillayute Airport and Forks post offices. The Forks post office at that time was located next to the old Ruel and Vedder store. Between the two jobs she worked full time.

Here On the Home Front

Social Life

After the bombing of Pearl Harbor and with most young men off to war the social life here on the Peninsula changed almost overnight.

Edna (Gentry) Leppell of Forks remembered one particular Saturday night when she was 12 years old her and her brother Don Gentry were dropped off at the Olympic Theater in Forks to take in a movie. Her mom and step dad were to play cards while Edna took her younger brother to the movies. Her folks had parked the car down town in front of Goffman's store next to where the big log is located today. After the show the two children would walk the one block from the theater to the car and by then her folks would usually be ready to go home. As the youngsters waited in the car two Navy men, probably from the Quillayute Air Base, happened by and according to Edna tried to get into the car. Edna was scared to death. "There was always a bunch of them in town on weekends," remarked Edna. Of course this wasn't typical of the servicemen's actions here on the streets of Forks during that time. Many of the military personnel were invited to homes for dinners and entertainment during their stay here in the West End as they were elsewhere around the Olympic Peninsula.

Marge Deinis and June and John Nelson remembered Clyde's Dance Hall located near the junction of Highway 101 and First Street in Port Angeles near where McDonalds restaurant stands today. After it burned down it was replaced with a smaller dance hall known as the Blue Danube. It was a popular place for dancing with the military that were based in the Port Angeles area during the war as well as being a favorite for many local families. There were also dances held at the USCG base out on Ediz Hook. According to June Nelson the Masonic Temple on Lincoln Street was another good place to dance.

Eleanor Thornton of Forks mentioned how, when they went to the theater in Forks, they would always leave the car keys in the ignition until one night after the show they found their car missing. Eleanor's husband Floyd found a young military boy driving it down Calawah Way just a block from the theater. The young fly boy was told not to be borrowing cars without the owner's permission and that was the end of that. The Thornton's had their car back and no law enforcement was needed.

Movie houses in Port Angeles were the Lincoln Theater on First and Lincoln, the Elwha on Front Street and the Olympian in the middle block of First Street. Marge and June remembered for entertainment they would go down to the Olympian, sit up in the balcony, put their feet up and watch the rats run about. John remembered an Eddy Clifford who used to play the organ at the Olympian. He was a famous organist and eventually went back to Seattle. June remembered when Van Johnson, the movie actor, was on stage at the Olympian. "There were about four of us girls there and we just set there drooling as we were only three or four rows up from the stage," said Marge

Marge also remembered Stan Boreson and his dog No-Mo coming to Port Angeles. Boreson, a Scandinavian humorist playing his accordion volunteered to entertain the U.S. troops as he visited 25 countries performing with the United Service Organization. Later Boreson and his dogs were featured on King TV's KING's KLUBHOUSE, A weekly children's show with music and humor.

John Nelson thought television came to Port Angeles in 1947 or 48 right after the war. Seattle's KRSC-V came on the air in November of 1948. This station later became KING 5. During the war they got their news from the radio or from news clips at the theater. They thought the news was maybe a month old before it was received at local theaters. They also remembered the Evergreen Dance Hall upstairs in a building near where the Peoples Store once stood.

John Leppell of Forks remembered watching the news clips prior to the movies at the Olympic Theater in Forks. He still recalls seeing the U.S. military shooting cannons in North Africa out in the desert and thinking what a dusty dirty place it was. He also remembered propaganda as when the enemy was captured and also the bombings. "Being young you didn't realize it was something real rather than just a movie," said Edna Leppell.

Bub Elvrum mentioned dances at Hunters Hall in Neah Bay across from where the Native American Vets cub is today. The hall was built by Jim Hunter back in the 20's according to Bub. At one time there was a place in the building to play basketball and Bub remembered the big pot bellied wood stove that heated the entire place. The building must have been 65 to 70 feet long at least and the Makah Boys big band orchestra played there for dances. Any of the military who could get the evening off came in for the entertainment. "There were a lot of young girls who could really dance well and they wouldn't miss a dance," said Bub.

It was supposed to be a "dry" reservation but at times the stuff flowed pretty well through there and the military boys would sometimes get themselves in trouble. "I know once a couple of our friends had gotten in trouble and got locked up. Well the word came down to the restaurant that they were in the Neah Bay Jail and they needed help getting out. So the boys' buddies went out and acquired a GI 6X6 at the base along with a cable and some chains and told the sentry they were going to go in and spring their buddies. Well they went in, hooked onto the jail door and got their buddies out. They finally lost the jail door somewhere on the way to the base. And sure enough here came the cop not far behind. Well the sentry guarding the main gate took three shots at the cop car, one going through the door, one through a window and one into the trunk as the Makah Law Enforcement was leaving," said Bub. The cop had seen enough bullets.

"The cop was a friend of mine. I got along with him fine. He was quite a guy. He decided that that was far enough to chase them when the bullets started flying," said Bub.

In Forks, Maynard and Pearl Lucken went to the Olympic Theater owned by the Fletchers every Friday night then over to the drug store for a milk shake. Real milk and ice cream back then you see.

WWII In Clallam County

In Carlsborg my mother remembered dances on Saturday nights at the Carlsborg theater and church. She remembered Rudolph as one of the bands that played there.

On May 8, 2012 following a West End Historical Society meeting I had the privilege of interviewing Gladys Allen, Joelene Wittenborn and Lee Gorham, all Forks residents who were in the Forks area during WWII.

They smiled and laughed as they spoke of the US. Navy, Army and Coast Guard personnel coming to Forks on the weekends to take in a movie at the old Olympic Theater or to visit bars, lounges, dances, the roller rink and more. The girls remembered a bus "The Liberty" coming in from the Quillayute Air Base with a load of military men looking for a good time in this little frontier town. And what a time it was with dances at the Legion Hall located along Forks Avenue across from where Sully's drive in is located today. And down town there were the Antlers Cafe and Lounge, and the IOOF building as well as the various taverns. The girls also reminisced on the fun days of roller skating at the Legion Hall. Oh, there were the occasionally fist fights in the parking lot and of course moonshine was available. The military had their own law enforcement, however, and would usher the bad boys back to the base. Overall, however, good times were had by most that turned out for those weekend social gatherings. The military, according to the three ladies was also invited to community dances such as the Senior Ball and the Firemen's Ball.

Dancing also took place at the Quillayute Grange Hall which

Here On the Home Front

was once the Quillayute School Gym located just east of the Quillayute Air Base. One of the local bands back then consisted of Betty and Chuck Palmer, Dr. Baker, Will Slather and Lloyd Wahlgren. The Fletcher band also played prior to and after the war. In an interview with Fred Shaw he also mentioned dances at the Beaver School Gym mentioning the music of Art and Betty Munson.

Well the old Olympic Theater burned down as did the Antlers Cafe, and dance hall, and the IOOF building burned in October of 2012. The Legion Hall fell victim to a heavy winter snow, the taverns gradually closed after the "Spotted Owl" controversy and the Quillayute Grange Hall was torn down as the structure began to diminish. Those old gathering places are sure to bring back memories, however, to those who visited here during the war years. Here in Forks. *Here on the Home Front.*

Warren Paul thought that one of the interesting things out here in Forks was that some of those in the military married local girls then stayed in Forks or returned to Forks after the war to settle down.

Myron Simmons spoke of school sports during the war when Forks would only play a couple games with Neah Bay and Clallam Bay then maybe district games in Port Angeles, Sequim or Port Townsend. "We didn't travel clear to Castle Rock like they do now, "said Myron. We also played intramural games. When the Navy came to Quillayute they would come in and play football and basketball against the Forks high school. La Push would also bring a basketball team to play Forks.

Jackie and Myron Simmons also mentioned the old skating rink located in Forks at 221 N Forks Ave. just across from where Sully's Drive In sits today. "We spent hours and hours and hours and skated miles and miles and miles at that old skating rink. That was fun there at the Legion Hall," said Jackie. They also held dances and later installed a bar and pin-ball machines. There was a meeting room in the front and also one upstairs.

Viola Holman remembered while living in Carlsborg she would go down to Dungeness and dance with the soldiers at Duncan's Tavern. My mother Vay (McHone) Dunlap-Archibald also remembered Duncan's as her and my father Delbert "Nig" Dunlap would work in Bugge's Cannery until eight or nine p.m. then go there dancing. "We would get there at about intermission. A lot of people went and they had good music," said mother. Mother also remembered dancing at the Fairview Grange Hall located between Port Angeles and Sequim "There were always a lot of soldiers and sailors there. There were a lot of good places to dance with good music back during the Big War, *Here on the Home Front*," said mother.

Virginia Dickinson of Dungeness recalled the Rudy's band playing at the old Dungeness Tavern on the weekends. "Some of the local farmers would dance then head home at closing time to milk the cows before going to bed," said Virginia. Many of the military boys camped on the Dungeness Spit would come across in boats at high tide, tie up to the dock and walk up town to dance. Virginia also mentioned the night in which two women, May Duncan and Betty Eberle drowned when the car in which Betty was driving went off the dock there at Dungeness. "What

Here On the Home Front

happened was there were a whole bunch of military boys stationed on the Dungeness Spit and they had a radio operation there. The soldiers and Sailors would come by boats to the dock, tie up to the float then walk up town to the tavern to hang out, dance and stuff. Virginia's mother, May and Betty had just came back from a show and the three women decided to take the soldiers back to the dock so they wouldn't have to walk so far. Mother got out of the car as she said there were too many people in there for her. When the car reached the curve on the dock it went off into deep water. The two soldiers got out and tried to get May and Betty out of the car but the two women drowned. It was thought that Betty, who was driving, had complained about chest pains and may have had a heart attack," said Virginia. At that time the dock went out about a half mile with a warehouse at the end. "That was quite the parking spot for all the lovers," said Virginia.

There were also those who traveled to visit during the war such as the case with my mother who made the bus trip from Carlsborg to Seattle with her cousin Toots (Feight) Cays of Sequim. Toots's husband Glen Cays was on his way to war. My mother Vay and Toots spent the night in a Seattle all-night theater. Glen left the next day and the women took the train to Spokane, then by train to Kooskia, Idaho to visit relatives. "Lots of soldiers on the train," said mother. Mother on her return trip took the train back to Seattle, then the bus to Long Johns Corner and walked home from there to Carlsborg. And what a walk that must have been with no traffic while passing alfalfa fields, irrigations ditches and pasture lands full of Meadowlarks.

WWII In Clallam County

Pete Capos spoke of the American Legion located next to where the Lamonts and Gottschalks stores once stood in Port Angeles.

According to Pete this was once called the Crescent Club and he was asked by a committee to set up the American Legion there and to manage it and so that he did. It was up on the third floor with apartments below. It opened on November 11, 1946. "We had music there twice a week and I used local musicians. We had a good musician who stayed here in between his circuits as he liked Port Angeles. His name was Van Ferguson who belonged to the Elks and had his own band. 'We had a bar and cocktail lounge with a dance floor." Filion was another band Pete remembered playing there and at other Port Angeles dance halls. My step father, Don Archibald played piano for Filion and other Sequim and Port Angeles bands in the forties and fifties. "People enjoyed the music. In the meantime we had a jukebox and I always made it a point to have all the best records on there. When we didn't have a band we had good dance music. All of Glen Miller's music was on that jukebox," said Pete.

Betty (Pedersen) Bernier of Forks also remembered her Mother Ada playing the accordion along with Ed Burr who played the Jews Harp, Ivy Price who played the fiddle, and mandolin and Ken Price playing the banjo for dances at the Beaver Community Hall which was located along what today is the Tyee Ridge Road. They also played at the Loop Tavern. Glen Price of Forks also remembered Ken Price playing for dances at the old Wilson place on the lower Bogachiel River across the swinging bridge.

Here On the Home Front

"Old Blonde Streeter, we just called him Pop, would meet us at the door of the IOOF Hall during dances that our folks were attending. Our parents would take us along and would have to check us in. Blonde would stamp our arm and we were never to leave until our parents were ready to take us home," said Betty. The children would often sleep on the benches at the IOOF until their folks were ready to go home back in those days. Another musician not mentioned before was Marge Cowan's brother Wally McDonald who played beautiful saxophone for the various dances.

Betty also mentioned the skating rink which was in the old Legion Hall across from where sully's Drive-Inn stands today. "Wayne Kritter's mom and dad Bill and Nan ran the skating rink and we would go rent skates and skate all night or until we couldn't stand up. You would skate to carnival style music," said Betty.

Betty also mentioned picking up beer and pop bottles with her friends then cashing them in and her dad would take them all to the movies in Forks. "Dad told us if we had enough money he would take us. He had an old green pickup and us kids would climb in the back, cover up with a blanket and off we went to Forks to the Olympic Theater. They wouldn't let you do that today," said Betty.

Glen Price of Forks mentioned family members who once played for local dances such as his brother Ken who played banjo and his mother Ivey who played accordion, pump organ, mandolin, and fiddle. She played at the Beaver community hall, the Loop Tavern in Beaver and also the Old Wilson place on the lower Bogachiel.

There was a large living room there at Monte Wilson's and a bedroom where we kids would conk out until the dancing was done," said Glen. Then they would all head back across the old swinging bridge, then to the La Push Road and back to Beaver.

Glen remembered as a kid growing up in Beaver along with the Loushin boys. "We were just kids and we dug fox holes along the railroad tracks as we thought we were going to be attacked by the Japs, Fred and Jim and I," said Glen.

Glen never ran out of something to do for entertainment as a child during the war years. "We didn't have any trouble finding something to do. When payday came Dad always bought us a carton of 22 shells to plink around with. By the time the two week pay period was gone we had those shot up and he bought more," said Glen.

"One of our favorite things with dad was when the Salmon Berries got ripe we would go over the hill to the Flu-Harty and start fishing the Dickey River, stay overnight then come out at the Mina Smith place near the little Quillayute Prairie. That was a real treat for us kids. No sleeping bags, we would just lay down by the fire and go to sleep. We would eat trout and if you got a hold of a steelhead you didn't have time to fool with them so you would just jerk the line and get rid of the fish.

We also spent a lot of time swimming at Lake Pleasant. Dave

Here On the Home Front

Smith, the tug boat operator on the lake, use to get mad as he would go chugging along with the tug pulling a raft of logs and we would swim out and get on that raft and he would be hollering at us to get off," said Glen.

Glen also remembered listening to the news every night on the radio and soon as the news was over the radio was turned off. On the weekends we got to listen to the Lone Ranger and them or if there was a boxing match on we got to listen but we didn't just turn it on and play it," said Glen. It ran on batteries you see. Glen also recalled that the Price family would save up enough gas coupons to allow them a once a year trip to Olympia or Mount Vernon to visit relatives.

Ed Duncan who lived on the Quillayute Prairie during the war spoke of not being able to travel much. Gas rations and cost were concerns. The Duncans, Wentworths, Maxfields, Parkers and Smiths did a lot of fishing and hunting both for recreation and food there on the Prairie. Colby Creek and the Dickey River were two fishing streams close to home for trout, steelhead and salmon.

Eunice Jones who operated the Joyce General Store with her husband Alton during the last year of the war remembered driving to Dry Creek near Port Angeles to attend dances She didn't remember any dance hall in Joyce at that time although there was a community hall.

Ernie and Joelene Wittenborn told of Forks having "Smokers" boxing matches. They mentioned Duke Streeter, Claude Clark and Frank Fletcher boxing when they were quite young. They fought at the old dance hall at Old Beaver.

Walt Fuhrman of Forks, as a kid liked to ride his bike and one day while riding down Fuhrman Road south of Forks he heard a P-38 go over him about a hundred feet off the ground and it scared him so bad he ran into a barbed wire fence. "It scared the heck out of me," said Walt. Walt's wife Adria remembered while playing when she was only five and diving under the steps of her home on Iverson Road whenever she heard a plane go over because she thought the Japs were going to bomb her. There was much uncertainty you see.

Joelene (Goodie) Wittenborn remembered her dad, Pa Goodie setting up a canteen out at Sappho where his tavern was for the servicemen. The guys would go out for eats and entertainment. "I remember one letter my dad had gotten from the parents, and I think the kid was killed, telling him how much they appreciated what he had done for their son," said Joelene. This was just one of many letters he received from servicemen and parents commending him for his thoughtfulness.

Jack Olson of Forks remembered while attending the Quillayute Grade School, there near the airbase, how he and Ed Duncan would go out at noon and fly their home made kites. When the wind came up at noon time we would get our kites up, tie them to a fence post then go back to school," said Jack. Every once in a while they would look out to see how those airborne flying contraptions were doing and every so often they would see them hit the ground. The wind would pick up and they needed

Here On the Home Front

longer tails you see.

Virginia (Huling) Blomgren of Forks who graduated from Forks High School in 1940, told of her social life in Forks during the war. "Fletchers Olympic Theater was a favorite place for teenagers to bring their dates. There were six of us kids out at Huling's Mill south of Forks at that time and at least four of us would come in to the movies on the weekend and after the movie we would go across Forks Avenue to Slim and Dell's cafe located where Starks True Value is located today. Of course we enjoyed the drug store and enjoyed going there during the day. They had a soda fountain and my cousin Darla used to jerk sodas there," said Virginia. It was called "Jerking Sodas" because of the jerking action the server used in moving the Soda fountain handle while making the soda. The drug store was located across from the movie theater on the corner of Forks Avenue and East Division. Joe Blomgren also mentioned the Cherry Coca Cola's that were made there.

Bob and June (Doran) Bowlby of Clallam Bay remembered going to Albert Fernandez's theater on Thursday and Sunday nights as it only ran two nights a week. They would show the news reels of the war. "It took a while to get the news over here in the states," said Bob. "Everyone listened to the radio and you got the city news pretty quick," said June.

"But I remember how frightening it was because I would have nightmares when we started getting the news about the Japanese planes and seeing that rising sun on the planes. I remember dreaming and having nightmares about them coming over and bombing Sekiu and bombing us," said June.

For some Sequim teenagers their social life was that of cruising the streets of Sequim. One Sequim school student wrote for *The Ditchwalker* publication of May, 2005:

> "Cruising The Strip" We cruised Sequim in our cars in the '40s and "50s. The strip started on the main drag at the VFW - Co-Op intersection, then through the one and only blinking red light to the next intersection where Kettel's 76 station is now located. That is a short two blocks with a U-turn at both ends, and we went really slow, no racing, three or four cars sometimes. I don't know why we were out there cruising at 10 p.m. because there was nobody on the streets to watch us. We'd cruise even if we were the only car. We even managed to cruise the town during the war with gas rationing down to two or three gallons per week.
>
> Some of the gas that was supposed to be used in farm tractors may have trickled its way into our cars. Two blocks and a U-turn. Two blocks and a U-turn.

John Jarvis of Agnew mentioned dances at Finn Hall which was a community hall located there near his farm on Finn Hall Road. The hall and the road are named "Finn" as when John was little this area was a Finnish community.

Bert Fletcher mentioned his parents Olympic Theater in Forks doing quite well during the war as sailors from the Quillayute Air Base would come to town to take in a movie and they would be lined up clear around the block waiting for the doors to open. "Pop corn was the only concession we had as chocolate candy bars were hard to get," said Bert.

Here On the Home Front

I found the following writings from June Robinson's column "Back When" 3rd page of the Peninsula Daily News Thursday August 28, 2003. And I quote:

From Prohibition to WWII, Clyde's was the place to be.

Once upon a time-76 years ago , to be exact-Clyde McDonnell opened the doors of a new dance hall on the east side of Port Angeles, Clyde's. To judge from the enthusiasm with which readers responded to last month's photograph, Clyde's Dance hall left a lasting impression on several generations of teens and young people of the North Olympic Peninsula.

Segee Capos of Port Angeles, who signed herself as "Clyde's most loyal dance fan!" wrote a long letter extolling "my memories-the most wonderful years of my life! Dancing was my whole life, and Clyde McDonnell made it a paradise for me!

"From 1928 until 1946, I never missed a dance night and never missed a dance any night that he was open. "He ran a decent dance hall, not rough house, and had the best music around at that time. "Puckett's was a great local band, and Clyde used to bring in many great bands from around the Seattle area, such as Dick Parker. Just about all of the big name bands came for one night at the time, including Ted Lewis, Phil Harris, Buddy Rogers, Roy Rogers, Anson Weeks and Ted Fio Rito. The dance hall would really be packed on those nights. There was a $1 entrance fee for a big- name band, otherwise it was 75 cents, and ladies were free if we got there before 9 p.m. "I was always there, as I would be picked up, with other 'regular' girls by Clyde at the corner of Laurel and Front, by the bank. After the first few years, after the dance., he drove us home right to our doorsteps, unless we had a date and had our own way home. When the sailors were in town, especially during the summers when the fleet would be here for three months and when any special ships of the Coast Guard ships came to town, there was always a special dance night. When the fleet came to town, Father would always meet with the vice admiral and tell him about the dance hall. They would arrange to give liberty to a certain number of sailors, and Father would send one of Wolverton's buses to pick up the sailors and return them to the dock."

"After a while, Father seemed to slow down and sold Clyde's. Those were some good days."

It was also stated in June's column that the military after taking over the hall during the war would move their cots on Wednesdays, Fridays and Saturdays to make way for the dances.

Myron Spath of Sequim remembered being there on V-J Day, September 2, 1945, when he was home from boot camp and a big name band, maybe that of Louis Armstrong, was playing. Doug McInnes of Sequim wrote that his older brother Rex, known as "Bud," went to the local dances, including Clyde's, on Saturday nights. "I remember my mother asking if he needed money. His answer was usually, 'I could use four bits or six bits. We have had a little inflation since the 1930's."

The following owners, Vern Burton and the Bowers family, named it the Blue Danube and later it was named Chubby's.

Out west in Forks Sisters Dorothy (Dankert) Barker and Ruth (Dankert) Zinter were grade school children and remembered the movies with the Lone Ranger, Gene Autry and Roy Rogers being their favorites. They also spent much time at the skating rink which was in the old Legion Hall. The soldiers and sailors would come and skate with us and visit with our parents," said Ruth.

Ed Duncan remembered that in 1944 Quillayute Union High School in Forks only played basketball games against Neah Bay, the Clallam Bay Signal Corps, Clallam Bay High School, Forks Cavalry, and Sequim which was played in Port Angeles. At the

Here On the Home Front

end of the season what was left of the Quillayute Union High School team consolidated with the Forks Town team to form a team in the Independent League. The football season was dropped because of the transportation situation and lack of man power. Many young men joined the military service. There were, however, a few turnouts. The Seniors and Freshman played the Sophomores and Juniors in two intramural games. The class of 1945 also played the Quillayute Air Base crewman in basketball as well as the Quileute Indian Nation, Clallam Bay, Neah Bay, and Port Angeles.

John Jarvis spoke of this old Finn Hall in Agnew being used for dances during the war. Photo by Lonnie Archibald 2014.

Wings Cigarettes

Wings Cigarettes were produced by Brown and Williamson Tobacco Company in the 1940's. The cards contained photos of 1930's and 40's aircraft with description and history of each plane on the back. Each pack of Wings Cigarettes contained one card. A series of 50 plane pictures and description were printed.

The Wings brand produced by Brown & Williamson was made available to American smokers in 1929. It was a ten cent economy brand packaged in a dark brown label. Do to wartime ink restrictions the Wings package gave way to white. The cigarette was also increased to king size about the same time. The plane cards measure 2.5 X 1.75 inches.

Supposedly these cards were printed during WWII although paper rationing occurred. Perhaps some were printed prior to the war then distributed during the war.

Wings cigarettes were produced in the 1940's with aircraft cards included in the package. From the collection of Greg Munson.

Here On the Home Front

These are examples of the airplane cards that were packaged with Wings cigarettes. From the collection of Greg Munson.

WWII In Clallam County

Scrap Metal Drives and Recyclables

George Wood of Port Angeles remembered the scrap metal drives. "First of all they wanted us to check in all the aluminum pans we didn't need and so the wife took an inventory and said, 'we can do without this and without that', and there was a wrecking yard down here and a lot that had been donated to the government for these aluminum pans," said George. The Woods took the pans down there and there was a pile of the pans "as tall as this Port Angeles Senior Center," according to George anyway. "I don't know what ever happened to those pans but they were there all through the war," remarked George. Oh I guess there were many items that made the recyclable list such as iron, copper, lard, grease, bacon fat, string, rubber and tin. They were doing their part for the war effort here in Clallam County, *Here on the Home Front*.

Lawrence Gaydeski remembered that when his uncle Joe Gaydeski was fire warden for the State Forestry out at Beaver he would bring home old rotten fire hose. They found they could make a cut around the edge of the canvas and rip the rotten canvas off leaving rubber to recycle. Of course the manufacturing of synthetic rubber really took off during the war helping to meet the needs of the war effort. Lawrence also remembered while living on the farm along the Sol Duc they would get a penny a pound for old rubber tires.

Ron Shearer remembered how in Forks they gathered up every bit of rubber and aluminum they could find. "They had aluminum drives and people would give up their aluminum pots

Here On the Home Front

and pans. I remember in the back of my dad's Shell station they rigged up a hoist to unload those big old solid rubber truck tires with cast iron wheels. They could then chisel the rubber off the wheels. Freight trucks would occasionally come by and haul the prized rubber and scrap iron away," said Ron.

Adria (Kaemmle) Fuhrman remembered during the war, while living north of Forks on Iverson Road, visiting the Wallace family. There was a big closet where they kept safety pins, mercurochrome, and iodine and we would tear up old sheets and roll them into bandages and it would stay in that big closet in case of a bombing. I was about five then," said Adria.

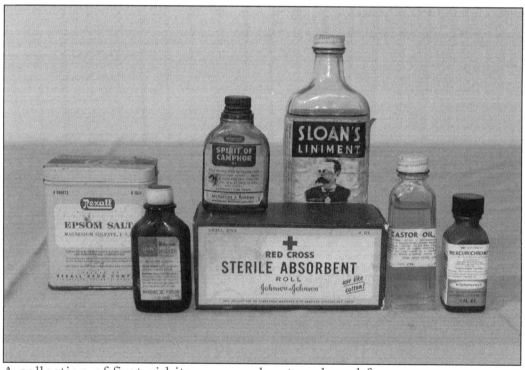

A collection of first aid items were kept on hand for emergency needs. Adria Fuhrman collection.

Adria also remembered peeling the aluminum foil off the individually packed chewing gum sticks and rolling it into a ball for recycling. Adria also remembered families saving balls of string.

Bob Bowlby spoke of the Welkers who had a flat bed truck there in Clallam Bay and the Boys Club needed money for various projects so they would pick up scrap metal in which they would receive a certain percentage of the sale after turning it in. With all the industry around Clallam Bay at that time it was rather easy to find scrap metal. Glen Willison had borrowed the truck from Walker's one day and they went out to the Cowan Farm on the Hoko-Ozette Road, now a State Park, and were told to go up Little River and take whatever they could find. We got a whole truck load of scrap metal up there then went up to an old gravel pit and found some railroad rails which was really prime stuff," said Bob.

Bob also told this story. "Another time we went up to the Cowan farm and when Cowans needed a new car they didn't wear out their old one they had it overhauled and it would be just like new. And there was a wonderful Model "T", a real classic, and they said go ahead and take that Model "T" for the war effort. And holy cow, I just cringed and drooled at the same time. I went to Glen Willison and told him that Cowan had given us a car and that I would replace it with equal scrap metal if I could have it. Glen said he knew they wouldn't go for that. We had towed it to the football field and the next time I went into Clallam Bay there was that car in pieces.

Here On the Home Front

What a wonderful old car that would have been. They came and hauled it off with the rest of the scrap metal," said Bob.

Steel War Pennies

There was a day back in the post war years of the 40's and early 50's while living in Carlsborg, I would pull my wagon along highway 101 from the Mill Road west to Rosand's Corner then north along Carlsborg Road to the Carlsborg Store where I would either sell or trade in the beer and pop bottles I had collected along the way. Not much traffic back then, you see. After leaving the store I would travel back south to Runnion Road, east to Mill Road, south to Gupster Road then east to Gilbert Road then south to Long John's Corner. It was there that John Gilbert would reward me with perhaps a jar of fish eggs and hooks and sinkers or with cash for the bottles I had managed to collect along the back roads of this farming country here in the Dungeness Valley. I would then head west along Highway 101 to home with wagon in tow. What bottles I found on this journey I would trade to Art Rosand the next trip back around. The cash at times would include a steel penny or two.

These 1943 steel pennies minted in San Francisco, Denver and Philadelphia came about due to a shortage of copper. Copper was needed for the WWII war effort. The production of the copper pennies came to a temporary closure for that year only. Instead pennies made of steel coated with zinc were minted. It has been reported that the savings in copper accounted for the making of many boats, planes, guns and nearly one and a half million artillery shells for the large guns. When minting began on the 1943 steel pennies about a dozen copper blanks were left in the minting machine and so somewhere there may still be a few of these 1943 copper rarities.

Here On the Home Front

Due to the coins often being mistaken for dimes and the fact that the pennies were stopped in vending machines by magnets which were in place to pick up steel slugs a public outcry occurred and the steel penny was eliminated by 1944.

John Leppell of Forks mentioned that his dad John, Sr. had quite a time with steel pennies while operating the State Liquor store in Forks. Pretty near all the liquor prices came out in odd numbers hardly ever rounded off to the nearest nickel requiring pennies for change. When the steel pennies first came out they were often mistaken for dimes when exchanged between the dealer and the customer. Due to all the confusion he started placing any steel pennies he received into a box saving them for his daughter. When years later they finally rolled the coins to take to the bank there was probably about 200 pounds of the unwanted steel coins. Most were in very fine condition. They traded them in at a penny a piece and soon after they become collectors' items.

After that Johnny and his wife Edna started collecting them for themselves as did many others. Today they are worth about a dollar each.

Tax Tokens

Here in Washington State we began using tax tokens in 1935. Dorothy (Smith) Burr of Forks remembered during the war when her father Leroy Smith had the Bogachiel Store south of Forks the soldiers would bring in tokens and she collected the coins from the various states. She was attending school at that time and helped at the store after hours. Dorothy remembered that three tax tokens equaled one penny. Some tokens were made of plastic and some of aluminum. I still have a green Washington State token and a red one from Missouri.

Ron Shearer remembered the tokens also. "When they first came out they were aluminum five to a penny then they needed more revenue and they were three to a penny. Then the aluminum was needed for the war effort and so they made them out of green plastic and they were still three for a penny," said Ron.

Tax tokens were to be used to pay for a tax that during the war was a one third of one cent. If one bought candy for 10 cents the merchant was to pay the State of Washington one third of a cent. Since charging the customer a penny for the ten cent purchase would amount to a 10 per cent tax the customer would instead give the merchant a tax token worth the one third cent. What a hassle for all involved.

John Jarvis of Agnew mentioned that the metal tokens also served as washers.

Here On the Home Front

Washington State sales tax tokens, worth 1/3 cent toward payment of sales taxes.

War Time News

Lawrence Gaydeski remembered during the war on Friday nights taking in movies at the Olympic Theater owned by the Fletchers in Forks. "Of course you would go to the show on Friday nights and they always had a news reel there showing some of the fighting going on especially the naval fighting and one thing or another and you would see those ships all shot to hell and it would keep you aware of it. And every day in the Seattle paper they had a list by name of the battle casualties and those wounded and missing in action. It kept people aware that things were not all good," said Lawrence.

Dorothy Burr also remembered getting some news from school in their "Weekly Reader". According to Dorothy they would discuss the war situation and even debate it in Debate Class.

Ron Shearer of Forks who was 13 during the beginning of the war delivered the Seattle PI and one of his friends delivered the Seattle Times. Yet another of his friends delivered the old Seattle Star. Ron covered the seven miles with his bicycle. During the week he made his route after school. Sometimes on a rainy Sunday he could talk his mother into driving him. Ron claimed that the war news however was only that which the government wanted you to hear and not much more. The news had been printed the night before so the paper was pretty much up to date.

Also out at Quillayute Air Base in April of 1944, "The

Here On the Home Front

Quillayute Quill" newspaper was set up and a copy was sent to the Secretary of the Navy for approval. After no answer a second request was sent in September and by October the request was approved and a six- sheet publication was printed.

Bert Fletcher, who's folks owned the Olympic theater in Forks remembered his mother Estene receiving war news reels on a regular basis. "I remember one reel showing General Patton. It came on saying this is General Pistol Packin' Patton and it went on about his accomplishments during the war. The Germans were scared to death of him," said Bert.

Bert also mentioned that General MacArthur was also often in the news reels. Bert also mentioned the local news in the Forks Forum which came out every Thursday and was published by Jim and Mami Astel.

WWII In Clallam County

Copies of Seattle newspapers, including the Star and Post Intelligencer, show headlines from the war in Europe and the Pacific. Gerry Archibald collection.

Here On the Home Front

Wreckage of the Lamut

Ron Shearer of Forks mentioned how his mother was always inviting servicemen to their house to hang around and eat with the family. "She would mother them as many were lonely. This one soldier from back east named Porky Swank was a regular around the house and was on the Beach Patrol stationed at La Push," said Ron.

It was April 1, of 1943 that Swank and another serviceman were patrolling Second Beach south of La Push when they came across a woman's body lying on the beach and that was the first indication that there was a ship in trouble. The two patrolmen started looking around and down near the end of the beach at Teahwhit Head was a ship hung up in the rocks. They hurried back to La Push and reported what they had found. It has also been said that the ship had sent out a distress call which was received at the La Push station. The USCG couldn't make the rescue by sea due to a very violent storm with winds reaching as high as 75 knots. They therefore attempted the rescue from a cliff above the Russian steamer that carried a crew of 44 men and 8 women. These servicemen were actually a search and not a rescue team and not equipped with the normal rescue equipment necessary in a situation as this. After cutting a trail through thick underbrush and trees and making their way along the jagged rocks the rescuers tied gauze together, which they had in their first aid kits, then tied the gauze to shoe laces to make a longer line and with a rock tied at the end of the gauze were able to throw the line to the freighter and eventually pull up a large rope from the ship's crew which was then secured and used as a life line. One at a time the ship's crew made their way up the rope to safety. It was said to be a very heroic rescue by the USCG. The women found on the beach was later identified as Koshova Alexandra, a 19 year old Russian who had been hit in the head by an oil drum and knocked overboard when the crew attempted to launch a lifeboat in the darkness and the storm along this wilderness coast line.

It has also been said that Russian ship captains who lost their ships would be put to death as punishment. Many of the individual Americans who were involved in the rescue and those who knew the dangers of this wilderness coast line wrote to Premier Stalin asking that the captain not be punished.

It is thought that these letters might have been responsible for the saving of the captain's life on his return to Russia. Later investigation of the wreckage of the steamship Lamut disclosed the grounding due to a combination of two currents that caused the ship to go ashore. One current was due to the strong southeasterly gale and the other an unknown local current which constantly forced ships towards shore. This and a combination of strong winds and tides had proved disastrous for the Russian steamer Lamut.

Approximately ten years after the ship wreck. Del Huggins and Henry Andreason of Forks made their way through the tangled brush and trees to Teahwhit head where Del tied one end of a rope to himself and the other end to a tree rappelling down the jagged cliff to the site where he found a hand painted Russian teacup in a bucket wrapped in rags, a memorial object from 1943 and the Russian ship Lamut.

The 250 foot long ship was built by Great Lakes Engineering Works of Michigan and launched in 1919 into Lake Erie. The steamer was later purchased by the Russian Merchant Marines and named the Lamut. She was a freighter transferring cargo between the Soviet east coast and the American west coast.

A photo from shore on Teahwhit Head of the wreck of the Russian steamer Lamut in 1943.. U.S. Coast Guard Photo.

Here On the Home Front

Aerial photo of the wreck of the Russian Steamer Lamut in 1943 at Teahwhit Head, south of La Push, Washington. U.S. Coast Guard Photo.

Lamut Tea Cup

As told by Muriel Huggins.

About ten years after the ship Lamut capsized, Darrell Klahn and Del Huggins of Forks were flying an airplane along the coast when they noticed something inside of the cave near where the ship had wrecked. Soon after, Del and Muriel Huggins, their kids and friends Henry and Ethel Andreasan decided to try and explore it. They made one attempt in the pouring rain but it was too stormy to get to the top of the cliff. About one week later Del, and son Jerry and Ethel hiked in over a blazed trail that had been made by the USCG to the top of the cliff to remove the crew and an injured woman. They took two ropes. Del slid down a one inch rope about fifty feet to the cave and tied a bucket to the other smaller rope. There he found a mattress, probably for the injured women to lay on, a small life raft, a radio, a compass, a pair of men's shoes which were from a shop in New York, and a Russian cup wrapped in rags. The radio and compass Del sent to the top of the cliff by way of the smaller rope. Then with Jerry and Ethel pulling from the top, Del climbed back up the rope with the cup and the smaller items placed in a bucket. The bucket and shoes were left at the top of the cliff and the radio was packed out part way. They had always planned to return for the treasured goods but never did. They did however bring out the beautiful Russian cup in mint condition painted with brightly colored flowers. Muriel Huggins still has her cup today at her home in Forks.

Here On the Home Front

This ornately painted tea-cup was recovered from the wreck of the Russian Steamer Lamut. Photo by Lonnie Archibald.

Other Stories and Such

Bob and June Bowlby remembered preparing at school for possible Japanese bombing missions. "We took a trail out into the woods east of the football field where large trees had fallen and left depressions where the root wads had been and they made perfect bomb shelters, you might say. So we could huddle behind where the bombs would be falling and stay out ot the danger zone," said Bob.

Lewis Dey, Sequim High school class of '48 sent in a list of many possible future topics for the Sequim Alumni Association's Ditchwalker publication in July of 2009. The topics themselves make a pretty good story!

Army convoys go through town on the morning of December 8, 1941; Soldiers take over Sequim gym, sleep on tiered seats; Military stationed in Methodist Church, Masonic Hall and farm fields ; Coast Guard and Army patrolled beaches with dogs, and built machine gun nests on beaches' Foxholes dug and barbed wire strung in many areas, including school grounds; Blackout of lights both house and barn, cars used only parking lights at night; Flares dropped by patrol bombers (PBY's) in Straits' Local citizens volunteer for 'round the clock duty watching for enemy aircraft; Rationing started, ration stamps for sugar, tires, shoes,. Gasoline rationed with A, B and C card priority; Savings bonds and stamps sold to kids in school; kids taken on jeep rides to promote sales; Kids collect anything military : hats, insignias, pins, stripes, gas masks, training manuals; City- raised soldiers help some farmers with haying and other farm jobs; Soldiers

Here On the Home Front

invited to local homes for dinner; Dances held for soldiers; Several local girls marry those soldiers both during and after the war; Flights of American B-17 Bombers fly over, 50 to 100 in a group; New and fast P-38 Pursuit aircraft hedge-hopping over Sequim, one crashed near Sherbourne Road.

Another story published in the Ditchwalker in November 2009 was entitled "Soldiers In Sequim 1942." The following recollections are from Vic Van.

Bergen, a soldier who arrived in Sequim just a few weeks after World War II started in December of 1941. Vic, now living in New Jersey, had a letter in the Peninsula Daily News in 2008 and since then has written letters to Harold Edgington, class of '49.

> "I was with a squad of soldiers sent to Sequim to check out the possibility of preparing bridges in the area for demolition if the Japanese attacked. We lived in the high school gym. Sequim was a small community, and believe me the folks were very friendly and kind to us."

> "The first time we had a day off some of us took a hike out to Dungeness. A man was selling crabs for 25 cents each, and seeing only his sign, I told him that back in New Jersey we bought crab 10 to $1. He then pulled out a crab for me to see and asked, "Like these?" Wow, we fell over when we saw the size, our first look at a Dungeness crab. I also recall a dance hall called the Chicken Coop. A lot of wine was passed around there."

> "We discovered a nice coffee shop on the main drag run by a nice lady named Betty. She had a tiny teenager behind the counter named Rose but we all gave her the nickname of 'Widget' and it stuck. She seemed to like it anyhow." (Authors note: this must have been Betty Blake's cafe. The young girl may have been Rose Ryser, but her sisters June Matriotti and Betty Dunlap cannot confirm it. At other times this cafe was known as Bruno's, Butch's and Tripp's.)

"In early August of 1942, we got our orders to return to Fort Lewis. And I will tell you an interesting story; I was almost killed in Sequim at that time. We had to close the latrine and Red Wallace and I got the job. So with axes, we started to bang on the wooden toilet seats, a very difficult job. So Red suggested that we get some gas from the motor pool and burn the darn thing. Well, after pouring gas on the seats, Red lit up his pipe and then threw the match on the seats. Well, all the methane built up in the latrine let go in one big explosion and the seats went flying up into the trees. Imagine how my family would have been notified that their son was killed by a latrine in far-off Sequim."

"Your area was beautiful and we enjoyed staying there. We left in July 1942 for the Aleutian Islands of Attu and Kiska. What a change. How we admired your area."

A story told to me by John Jarvis of Agnew is that of one of Jarvis's cows being shot by mistake when soldiers were camped at John's family farm in Agnew. John recalled, "The sentry out there in the field at night time seen an object moving and said 'halt' and the beast kept on coming and he shot but it wasn't of Japanese descent, no, it turned out to be old Bessie, one of our best Guernsey's."

Here On the Home Front

The soldiers were camped on the Bucher Farm east of Brown Road in Sequim, circa 1942. They were curious about the cows because many of the young men were from the east coast & farm life was new to them. The soldiers spent hours at target practice in the back pasture to keep their skills sharp. Photo courtesy of Nellie Bucher from the Sutter-Bucher Estates.

Bert Fletcher added to the story told by Darrel Klahn and Lawrence Gaydeski of Forks on the subject of planes buzzing Forks High School during the war. "There wasn't a minute in the day that there wasn't a Navy plane flying over Forks for one reason or another and they would often buzz the school. That one previously mentioned wasn't the only one. We had our grade school buzzed as well. An F-2 Wildcat buzzed us and I could see the pilot in the planes window and the tires on the side of it and the stars on the windshield. He couldn't have been more than 50 feet above the school. A guy would be court marshaled for doing that now but they would do a lot of that. They would buzz the housing projects and buzzed my grandparents' house several times. The pilots seemed to be having a heck of a good time. Some people found it annoying but I thought it was just great. About a month after the war was over it all pretty much trickled out and all the planes finally went back to Sand Point Naval Air Station in Seattle," said Bert. Sand point was kind of a hub Navy base for this region. According to Bert, Quillayute was a hub, an auxiliary base as was Arlington, Whidbey Island and Shelton Washington.

Out east in Sequim Ross Flanders, class of '52 wrote for The Ditchwalker publication of May 2005 the following:

"Behind Every Tree."

> Nerves were jumpy right after the war started. I remember my dad and John Campbell saying, "If the Japanese attack it will be right through here." At age seven, to me that meant right through our farm. I was terrified to go out at night because there was an enemy behind every tree and we had many trees.

It was in June of 1942 that the 324 foot steamship "Coast Trader," a freighter carrying newsprint from Port Angeles to San Francisco, was torpedoed 37 miles southwest of Tatoosh Island off Neah Bay. The crew who took to a lifeboat and rafts was saved and taken to Neah Bay and Port Angles by the fishing boat "Virginia I" and the Canadian ship "Edmundston." One man died from exposure and several were injured as their ship was sunk. It was reported that the Japanese sub I-26 had torpedoed the freighter but it was also reported that the U.S. Navy denied being torpedoed and that it was an explosion within the freighter. But then one needs to take into consideration the fact that there was much propaganda on both sides during the war.

Shortly after the sinking, another Freighter "Fort Camosun" was torpedoed and shelled off Cape Flattery. There were no casualties and the steamer was towed to Neah Bay and eventually to Seattle.

Boyd Rupp mentioned the beginning of the building of a large fortification at Neah Bay. After the bombing at Adak, Alaska the military, although already on high security along the coast, was sure Clallam County would be attacked. Large guns with 16 inch bores were planned. According to Boyd, this was to be an underground fort. It was never completed as once the U.S. Military knew of the location of the Japanese and planned to invade Japan the coastal defense became somewhat more relaxed and the plans for a Cape Flattery fort were scrapped.

Yet there was another event told by Harvey Green which he remembered while in the 6th grade at Beaver School north of Forks; "On the school front, the usual fire drill was now accompanied by the "Air Raid Drill." These drills were conducted several times a week and were quickly organized into a serious, smooth working drill. As a 6th grader I was assigned four underclass persons to my squad. Each 6th grader was instructed on making sure that his/her group assembled at the predetermined spot and together they would run to the nearby heavily wooded area about 10 yards away, where they would hide. I had found an indentation in the nearby woods with a large moss covered log serving as a canopy over a portion of the indentation if an attack was in progress. I felt sure that we would be adequately protected. But today, I'm not so sure."

Betty and George Early of Clallam Bay also told of a B-17 crashing during the war on a ridge between Clallam Bay and Pysht above what has been called the coal mine. There were no reported casualties. It was years later that their son Cecil Early, Kirk Selfridge, and others hiked into the crash area from the Clallam Bay School. They found a few parts scattered along the hillside. There was also a rumor that a 50 caliber gun had at some time been removed from the scene and was found mounted on a fishing boat in Neah Bay. The owner of the boat got word that the government was coming to confiscate it and so he threw it overboard.

Yet another story told to me by John Leppell was the following: "Mickey Merchant of Forks found a bottle on a local ocean beach back during his beach combing days with a note asking whoever picked up the bottle to contact a certain address in Japan. Mickey did and they sent back a very detailed map of part of the Straits and the Pacific Ocean beaches stretching down as far as Grays Harbor. "It was very detailed with ocean depths, head lands, type of beach, islands etc.," said Johnny. From this map Johnny always thought that the Japanese knew what they would be getting into if they were to invade our rugged ocean beaches here on the Olympic Peninsula. Johnny

Here On the Home Front

remembered the map being on display in the old drug store in Forks for a number of years. He often wondered what happened to it. Johnny always wondered where the Japanese got the map. He also mentioned that there were a lot of Japanese along the coast prior to the war supposedly looking for gold. Darrell Klahn who also grew up in Forks wondered if those Japanese beach bums had something to do with the mapping.

I wish to publish another story handed to me by Dave Richmond of the upper Hoh Valley who is a grandson of John Huelsdonk, "The Iron Man of the Hoh." Beginning in 1928, Elizabeth (Huelsdonk) Fletcher and her husband John Fletcher built the Ruby Beach Resort located in west Jefferson County along the Pacific Ocean south of Forks. At the conclusion of the construction of the Ruby Beach Ocean Resort, the Fletchers owned a store with living facilities, a gasoline pump and fifteen cabins. In the spring of 1942 they were notified by way of a letter from the National Park Service that the government needed their land. The following is that which was written by Elizabeth.

> My husband, John, and I had a scenic resort at Ruby Beach, which might possibly be used as a base if the Japanese obtained possession. Japanese were seen quite often along the coast with camera in hand, pointing to some scenic spot. Most likely they were only doing so because the area had a beautiful view. In fact, someone scouted the coast with the idea in mind that the Japanese might find it just right for a base camp. One such expedition showed this to be foolish with the salal bushes ten feet high entangled and entwined among the spruce blowdown, the result of the powder post beetles. In fact, if one let himself down on the tops of the salal bushes, he would find himself ten to fifteen feet from mother earth--quite a comedown. He might find the need to crawl out on his hands and knees. Not really a good site for a base camp.

John and I were not even given a lease on our quarter mile ocean front and had to be content with $20,000. I remember the day that we left and the ache in our hearts. We were given two weeks to clean our cabins of housekeeping goods. There was no place to store our housekeeping furniture except in my brother's-in-law, Fred Fletcher's, barn. The army officer in charge kindly lent us the use of the army trucks and the job was complete in the two weeks' specified time. All they wanted left were wood burning stoves. I remember as we left, John seemed to share the agony of the situation and despair that I must be feeling. He said to me gently, "Don't look back, Bettine." The lovely place we had been so proud of was left beyond the bend of the highway. We had left Ruby Beach forever; but hope, useless hope, made the pain no less bitter.

NOTE: Family members today still wonder why the letter of eviction was sent to the Fletchers by the National Park Service rather than the US military. The author.

Here On the Home Front

Ruby Beach Resort, overlooking Abbey Island with Hoh Head in the distance. Forks Timber Museum collection.

Beverly Porter remembered while attending high school in Joyce she would walk over a mile each day to catch the bus. "My dad had built a bus stop shelter so that when it rained and snowed the children would have a place to set on a bench out of the harsh environment. They would also leave extra clothing there they didn't want to take to school that their mothers had made them wear. "My little sister Joan, Norman Stovall, Doreen Taylor and I were waiting in the school bus shack and the bus hadn't come but we heard this thundering sound and here came a whole contingent of mules the military was taking out to the west end and that was kind of exciting because all of these young soldiers were winking while pushing those mules ahead of them with the bus behind arriving about an hour late," said Beverly. And what a sight that must have been, like a Norman Rockwell painting with mules prancing, dogs barking, cats scurrying, birds flying and wide eyed children standing at attention along this little country road here in Joyce.

Here On the Home Front

Rumors and the Like

Frances Maxfield Quillayute Prairie told of a Navy cousin of her husband Art flying a plane down the Pacific coast in search of a Japanese sub that was trying to get in near here. Here meaning the north Olympic coast you see. When I asked Francis what she knew about that she replied "well I just know what they said. The relative, and we will call him Cyrus, said he was searching for a sub that was heading towards La Push. Cyrus never said much more than that as they never would tell you much during the war."

For me this brought back a couple stories I had written in my first book *THERE WAS A DAY* and told to me and Ron Shearer by retired WSP officer Boyd Rupp of Forks. According to Boyd, submarines would come into a cove at the mouth of Goodman creek just south of La Push to charge their batteries. Boyd also mentioned he saw four U.S. Hell Cat planes drop depth charges just off Waadah Island at Neah Bay. Two weeks later Coast Guardsmen remarked that two Japanese subs had been destroyed. A lot of book matches floated to shore and, according to Boyd, were from a tavern in Astoria, Oregon. "We had sympathizers who were supplying the Japanese with goods," said Boyd.

Also in the book is a story told by Ed Claplanhoo of Neah Bay who mentioned that a Japanese submarine was rammed by a US boat, The Black Douglas, which was stationed at Neah Bay during the war. He recalled bakery products found in the debris after the sub split and sank. The goods were from an old Port

Here On the Home Front

Angeles bakery known as "Palace's." Someone had been supplying the Japanese sailors. Ed also told of a German show house operator in Neah Bay who was suspected as being a spy. He was gone at war's end.

It was also reported that a Coast Guardsman working in a lookout station east of Neah Bay was found beaten and thrown over a cliff. The phone in the lookout had been ripped out. This incident occurred in March of 1942 and was unexplained. Was it a Japanese or perhaps a German or Japanese sympathizer? It was never explained.

According to Bob Bowlby of Clallam Bay the supposedly mining efforts by the Japanese prior to the war along our ocean beaches, mainly near Ozette, were just a cover up as what they really wanted was a good flat surface for landing planes. Bob also thought the Japanese had planned to land flying boats on Lake Ozette. Other rumors were that they were also mapping the area.

Yet another rumor Bob had heard was that during the war a telephone lineman working up a pole east of Pysht near Jim Creek along the Straits of Juan De Fuca had seen a Japanese submarine just off shore. He called it in but the crew had spotted him and left in a hurry.

Another rumor here on the North West corner of Clallam County was that of invaders at Cape Flattery west of Neah Bay. It was April of 1942 when an Army observer had reported the incident during the late hours of darkness. This was no doubt to become the beginning of an attack here on our shores as it was also thought that invaders were coming ashore south of Cape Flattery. To make the invasion even more believable the light at the Destruction Island lighthouse off Ruby Beach was reported out. Just moments after the report it was reported by a Sequim based Battalion to the Naval District in Seattle that they had received notice from Neah Bay that indeed landings of hostile forces had been made along those wilderness shores between Ozette and Neah Bay. Soon forces from Fort Warden in Port Townsend and Fort Lewis in Tacoma were on their way to defend the Coast from those invaders. Even Canada was ready for war against what was thought to be Japanese invaders.

After investigation by the USCG and Army no invaders were found and all was back to normal. Well as normal as could be during those war times here in Clallam County. *Here on the Home Front.*

In Sequim Doug McInnes mentioned trees felled and burned in bon fires arranged in a pattern thought by some to point the way to Boeing's in Seattle as a guide for Japanese bombers.

Here On the Home Front

Rumors Not Substantiated

According to a book entitled "The Phantom War in the Northwest and an account of Japanese Submarine Operations on the West Coast by Grahame F. Shrader there was a persisting belief that Japanese submarines entered Puget Sound waters during the war but nothing in official records-United State or Japanese, supported that belief. Also that there was no evidence ever found to support that theory.

According to writings by Bert Webber in his book "Silent Siege-If The Japanese did come to our coast and yes the freighter "Coast Trader" was sunk by a Japanese submarine. Webber also mentioned that the Japanese had submarines stationed along the U.S. Pacific Coast and had plans to attack lighthouses on Christmas Eve 1941. Webber also wrote that the orders were cancelled however.

There are documentations, however, of Japanese submarines attacking freighters carrying oil and lumber off the Pacific Coast ranging all the way from California to Alaska. Oil fields and lighthouses were also reported to have been torpedoed by submarines.

Here On the Home Front

WWII In Clallam County

A Letter from Pa

The following appeared in "Knickerbocker News" of Albany, New York in April of 1942.

Friend of Albany Sergeant Tells Folks 'All About Him'

A stirring example of how the war is helping to knit American's diverse population together was revealed today by John J Carey, and Myrtle, who has received news of their son, Sergt. John J Carey Jr, from a Washington State tavern owner.

Carey received a letter recently from J.M. (Pa) Goodwin, Sappho Wash. telling of young Carey's visit to the store and his conduct as a "perfect gentleman."

Goodwin wrote what the reason or his letter was, a desire to become better acquainted with the parents of the more than 600 servicemen who have "registered" at the tavern. His letter to Mr. and Mrs. Carey follows .

"I suppose you will think it's quite strange to be getting a letter from someone you have never seen or heard of, but it seems anything can happen nowadays so get set and brace yourselves." Your son, Sergt. John J. Carey, is soldering out in this part of the world. I made his acquaintance some time ago. He came into my place when he first landed here and has been in several times since."

"My place is a tavern on the main highway enroute to the camp where your boy is staying. I have a book that I use as a register, and we have over 600 names and addresses in it up to now."

"We serve the soldier boys coffee, sandwiches, doughnuts and cake free of charge. I have served about 60 pounds of coffee to them and do they love it. Your boy put on a show for us. About 50 people were present and when he played the part of the Hunchback of Notre Dame, he went over like a million."

Here On the Home Front

"I have been writing about six letters each day to the mothers and fathers of boys who come into my place, and I have been getting letters from all over the country. I have about 75 letters and cards now."

"I want to say your boy is a perfect gentleman. You have someone to be proud of in him. If you care to write to me I'll sure be glad to hear from you. Goodbye for this time."

In his answering letter, Mr. Carey thanked Pa Goodwin for his news of "Sergeant Jack."

"The nice things you said about him naturally pleased us," he wrote, "and I am sure the letters you have written to various parents about their sons were thankfully received. There are not many who would take the time to write to so many folks, and I am sure the good Lord will reward you."

The following is a letter sent to Pa Goodwin from John J Carey on April 13, 1942.

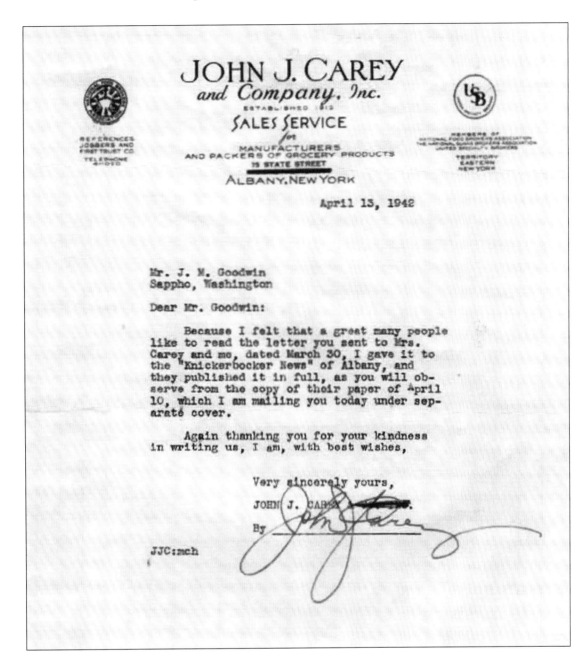

Letter from Joelene Wittenborn collection.

Here On the Home Front

VE and VJ Day "The War is Over"

VE Day, an important date to remember, is May 8, 1945 when the armed forces of Nazi Germany and Adolf Hitler's third Reich surrendered, ending the war in Europe.

VJ Day (Victory over Japan) is also known as VP Day (Victory in the Pacific Day). Japan surrendered in the afternoon of August 15, 1945, because of time zone differences was August 14, here in the States.

During VJ Day As a fifth grader in Forks Bert Fletcher was looking forward to his father Henry Lossen Fletcher coming home after serving in the South Pacific for two solid years as a Chief petty officer on a destroyer escort. His total time in the Navy was three years. When I asked Bert if he had witnessed any celebrating he made the comment that he remembered more so when the war in Germany ended. "I remember VE Day was in May and I was in the fourth grade at the time and the old fire truck was running south on the main drag through Forks blowing the horn and siren," said Bert. And what a sight that must have been on that clear day with dogs howling and children taking notice as that old fire truck made its way through town. Here in Forks. *Here on the Home Front.*

On August 14, 1945, Lawrence Gaydeski was with his dad near what is now the truck route overpass along highway 101 on the west side of Port Angeles. "That day was an interesting experience," remarked Lawrence. "I was 14 or 15 years old and just wandering around there that day as crews were surfacing the road. In those day's they didn't put black top down. They just poured oil down and laid gravel on it and spread it out. Well they had just poured oil there maybe a half mile long and they were ready to spread gravel and they had flaggers for one way traffic and all of a sudden the mill whistle in Port Angeles started blowing and drivers were so excited they started driving right through the oil which wasn't covered yet and the flagman, and I can't remember yet, but I think they were giving work permits to kids and Ed Duncan of Quillayute was one of the kids flagging there when drivers were going through with black oil just a flying as they were yelling 'The War Is Over, The War Is Over.' Well my old man ran down there to see what was going on and Ed was yelling 'I can't stop 'em, I can't stop 'em,' and he thought he was going to catch hell for it but the old man said to him 'what are you to do?' That was some experience," said Lawrence.

That was the day in which the initial announcement of Japans surrender was made. It was September 2, 1945 that the formal surrender ceremony took place on the battleship USS Missouri in Tokyo Bay.

Pearl Lucken remembered her husband Maynard working at Lake Pleasant shingling a house when she heard the news on the radio that the war was over. "I picked up Donna May Walken, drove to where Maynard was working and hollered to him the 'war is over, get off that roof,' then I drove into Tyee and called everyone I knew to come on to my house we were going to have a party." said Pearl. Well they got out what whiskey they had saved during the war, contacted Jackie and Dave Micheau who played piano and saxophone, moved back the furniture and danced and partied.

My mother remembered working at the Carlsborg store for Eldon Paulson and Chet Bombardier when the war ended. There was always a bottle kept in a drawer and it was to stay there until the war ended then it would be brought out for a drink. When the war ended someone came into the store announcing that the war was over and sure enough the bottle was removed from the drawer. "The day it was over, everybody was driving up and down the street in Carlsborg honking their horns and celebrating that the war was over," said mother.

Pete Capos of Port Angeles was on a Navy ship off Yorktown Virginia when they heard the announcement over the ships intercom that the war had ended. "Well that was great news so we got out a bottle of champagne to celebrate. That was on a Sunday evening and we would have a drink to the end of the war. We no sooner killed the bottle and another announcement came that it was not official, the war was not over when two days later we finally received word that yes the war was officially over," said Pete, and how happy they were as they returned to the Norfolk Navy Base in Virginia.

After the war Pete returned to Port Angeles. "We were lucky to survive a war like that," said Pete, "a lot of good guys never came home." He needed a suit and couldn't find one. "Couldn't buy anything after the war for a while. I finally went down to the Toggery and said as soon as you get some in please let me know," said Pete. "Well, the suits finally came, you see."

Here On the Home Front

At the Quillayute Air Base there was a short period of horns, sirens and the congratulatory handshakes but it has been said that this wilderness Air Base took the news calmly. A two day holiday was declared.

In Sequim Doug McInnes (class of '48) wrote in the "Ditchwalker", "We cruised Sequim in our cars in the '40s and '50s. The strip started on main drag at the VFW-Coop intersection, then through the one and only blinking red light to the next intersection. That is a short two blocks with a U-turn at both ends. I don't know why we were out there cruising at 10 p.m. because there was nobody on the streets to watch us. The biggest cruise in Sequim was V-J Day, in 1945. Everybody cruised the strip, even farmer Jess Taylor, founder of Sunland. Jess had the loudest horn, and other members of our parents' generation got caught up in the frenzy too. Phyllis McNamara broke the ring on her Studebaker car horn for hitting it too hard."

June Bowlby told of the day the war officially ended. "I think it was about early afternoon and the shop whistle in Sekiu blew and blew and blew and then we found out that the war was over. Everyone ran out into the street and they were yelling and celebrating," said June. It was Rayonier's shop located near where the treatment plant is today and Olson's dry camping spots. Bloedel sold portions of its holdings to Rayonier in 1945. June's husband Bob was in the Navy at dry dock in Bremerton as his ship was getting guns changed over when the war ended.

Harvey Green of Forks mentioned the following: "During the

summer of 1945 I was working for a wood cutter, splitting, and loading wood into a 1931 Model B Ford, "stake bed" truck. Our location of operation was about 20 yards on the south side of Highway 110, located between Highway 101 and the Quillayute air base. The old one cylinder drag saw was a noisy, rough running machine, and accompanied with the ring of the splitting ax, it was impossible to hear. As I looked up from the last cut on a 3 foot diameter block of wood, there was a lady in a blue 1940 Plymouth calling and motioning to us. The saw was shut down and the lady announced in a loud clear voice, "The war is over!" We immediately packed our gear and drove towards the little town of Forks. As we passed cars along the highway they flashed their lights, waved and honked their horns, it was all quite exciting.

As we entered Forks, the streets were clear of people by this time, but there was still general milling along the sidewalks where people were talking and laughing together-"post-war euphoria" was in the air. The War Was Over.

George Early of Clallam Bay also mentioned, as had Lawrence Gaydeski of Forks that he and Ed Duncan were working just west of Port Angeles near Fairmont oiling the road for the State Highway when they heard the mill whistles blow and the Navy boats shooting off their guns in the harbor. Ed said, "That's it, my brother Willey will be coming home from the war." "Everyone was celebrating" said George. *Here in Clallam County, Here on the Home Front.*

Here On the Home Front

Historic Background

On 3 September, 1945, a letter from the office of the Chief of Naval Operations was received at Naval Auxiliary Air Station, Quillayute, Washington, carrying the following information. "The maintenance of N.A.A.S., Quillayute in a full operation station is not now required due to the change in Aviation Planning Requirements.

Effective 15 September 1945, N.A.A.S., Quillayute will be reduced to a caretaker status, which includes preventative maintenance and protection of government property and there will be no aircraft operation at this station."

Thus, the sounds of war left the sky over the little logging town of Forks, Washington. Where once the familiar sounds of F-4F Wildcats, F-6F Hellcats, T.B.F. Avengers, P-38 Lightening and the slow moving, majestic K-type Blimps filled the sky--- there was silence. No longer would the "hot shot, lovesick" pilots buzz the Quillayute Union High School, creating havoc with the school day, giving the Principal fits and sending the girls into a dither. The sky over Forks returned to the prewar status, a brilliant deep blue, towering white cumulus clouds, the age old sounds of nature. And from the distant hillside, the staccato sounds of the "Whistle Punk" as he sent his message to the yarder. The world was at peace once more.

The prewar grass landing strip just south of Forks, had early on in the war been rejected by the Navy as an "emergency landing strip because of the lack of space for expansion." During

Here On the Home Front

the World War II years (December 7, 1941 to September 2, 1945) Civilian Aviation had been suspended, and nature had taken back its own, covering the Forks Airport with ferns, small fir and alder trees, tall grass and the ever present Scotch Bloom with its familiar yellow blossom .

Post war civilian aircraft production was soon under way. Such companies as Cessna, Piper, Aeronca, Taylorcraft, and Stinson were retooling and soon producing a variety of single engine light aircraft for market to a population that was war weary, ready and eager to embark upon the post war aviation boom. The war had produced a great number of experienced pilots and it was from this vast pool of airmen that the upcoming civilian pilots were to receive their flight training. The G.I. Bill of Rights, offered flying lessons to the veterans and this, along with America's fascination with the airplane would spawn many small flying schools, and grass airstrips would appear as quickly as the toadstools of the field.

Post War

Automobile manufacturers were hiring lots of help and were switching over from military to civilian production. You couldn't get a new car for a couple of years. You could get your name on the list, "said Darrell Klahn. "One of the things that happened here that was impressive to me and to others, I'm sure, was that a lot of people bought airplanes. I think we had thirteen airplanes in a community of only 600 people which we claimed was more aircraft per capita than any place in the country. And geographically you know it was a good thing out here," said Darrell. According to Darrell the Forks airport located where it is today was built by the CCC's in 1940. "After the war a man by the name of Bill Brandsfield moved to Forks and he taught us all how to fly." said Darrell.

John and Edna Leppell of Forks told of days in 1948 when they paid the government $200 to $300 for a 20 X 75 barrack in which they spent weekends pulling nails and tearing down at the Quillayute Airport. "That was a heck of a lot of money at that time," said Edna. "It was all number 1 lumber, no knots in it or anything," remarked John. It was all good material with no rot as the barracks had only been up for 4 to 6 years. The home I live in now on the Sol Duc River north of Forks once contained windows from the old Quillayute Air Base.

Ed Duncan remembered a Mr. Konopaski buying some of the Navy and Army barracks at Quillayute after the war and moving them to various areas. "They were big long buildings and they cut them in half. Some set over at Art Maxfield's on big prairie

Here On the Home Front

until they were sold." said Ed

WWII In Clallam County

Blue and Gold Stars

Betty Dunlap of Sequim still had a Blue Star which indicated she had a family member serving their country during the war. These stars were posted in store windows or homes. On the back of the Blue Star these words were written. "As A Token of Our Loyalty and Respect to The Member Of Your Family Who Serves In The Armed Forces Of America."

A Gold Star was posted for a family member killed during the war.

Blue Star posters signified a family member was serving their country during the war. Judy Stipe collection.

Here On the Home Front

This is of the author Lonnie Archibald on the porch of his Grandma Eva McHone's in 1944. Note the blue star on the window as his uncle Frank (Pete) McHone was fighting in Europe.

Memorials

In Forks the VFW is named after Walt Fletcher and Arthur Wittenborn, (Forks boys) who were killed in the war in Europe.

Fletcher Killed In Germany

First Lieutenant Walter Alvin Fletcher, husband of Mrs. Helen Fletcher of Forks was killed in action in Germany on April 15, 1945 according to a telegram received here on Friday, from the War Department. He was the second son of Mr. and Mrs. A. A. Fletcher, also of Forks.

Walter enlisted in the Army on August 28, 1942 and graduated from Officers Candidate School at Fort Benning, Ga., on April 24, 1943 as a second lieutenant. In August, 1944, he was shipped overseas and was there assigned to the 9th Army. Lt. Fletcher took part in the battles in France, Belgium, Holland and Germany.

Memorial services will be held at Forks Sunday, May 6, at the Legion Hall at 2:00 p. m.

Rev. Evan David of the Congregational Church will conduct the services.

Tribute to 1st Lt. Walter A. Fletcher

by his Commanding Officer, Capt. Donald H. Evenson. Excerpts from a letter written to Mrs. Walter A. Fletcher.

"To know Walt was to love him. I thank God that I was granted that privilege. His personality, his sense of humor, his sense of loyalty, his consideration for others, his general make-up endeared him to all who knew him. The platoon he loved, who loved him so well, men who have become hardened through battle, and to whom life is cheap, stood with tears in their eyes, shocked to the core, when they learned of their irreplaceable loss.

"Walt died as he lived, a man in every sense of the word. He gave his life so that all right thinking, freedom loving people on this earth might live unmolested, free from all harm. What more can be said of any man?

"The battle was a hard fought one. His last words to his platoon were, 'Come on, you fighting third, I love all of you.' They rallied to the man and were victorious in the end. Truly his memory will live as a shrine to those who are left to carry on."

Newspaper accounts of the death of First Lieutenant Walter Fletcher of Forks in 1943.

In Sequim the VFW is named after Henry Echternkamp who was killed in Pearl Harbor on the Arizona.

At Port Williams one can visit a memorial to Sequim's Marlyn Nelson who was killed in Pearl Harbor aboard the California.

Here On the Home Front

Sgt. Wittenborn Killed in Action

Staff Sergeant Arthur Wittenborn has been killed in action in the fighting in Europe. This was the shocking news received by his parents, Mr. and Mrs. Wm. J. Wittenborn, Monday night.

The family has received no other details, other than that he had been killed in action.

Sgt. Wittenborn had just been returned to duty in July following his recovery from injuries received in action several weeks previous. At that time he was in France and was removed to a base hospital in England.

Sgt. Wittenborn had been given the bronze star for meritorious achievement in the line of duty, and he was also the holder of the purple heart.

Sgt. Wittenborn attended the schools here and was a graduate of Quillayute High School. He has been in the army more than two years and overseas for more than a year.

Arthur was well known among his friends here as a great hunter and fisherman and was a great lover of the outdoors as well as a good athlete.

Arthur is survived by his parents, Mr. and Mrs. Wm. J. Wittenborn; his brother, Ernest; his grandmother, Mrs. A. B. Cameron; his uncle, Lefty Hays besides numerous other relatives and a host of friends.

The Federal Building in Port Angeles has been renamed the Anderson building after Richard B. Anderson of Agnew who was killed when he hurled himself on a grenade to save fellow Marines. For this he was awarded the Medal of Honor.

Also named for Anderson was the Destroyer RICHARD B ANDERSON built at the Todd Shipyard in Seattle in July of 1945. There is also a memorial to Anderson at Veterans Park in Port Angeles.

The Purple Heart medal awarded to Sergeant Arthur Wittenborn who was killed in action fighting in Europe. Joelene Wittenborn collection.

Here On the Home Front

Richard B. Anderson Memorial in Port Angeles, at the Veterans Memorial Park next to the Clallam County Courthouse. Photo by Lonnie Archibald.

Marlyn Nelson of Sequim was killed in Pearl Harbor on December 7, 1941. His memorial overlooks the bay at Port Williams near Sequim. Photo by Lonnie Archibald.

Here On the Home Front

Index

Agnew Community Hall, 19
Alexandra, Koshova, 232
Allen, Gladys, 203
Anderson, Art, 7, 80, 186
Anderson, Nanson, 189
Anderson, Richard B., 272
Andreason, Henry, 232
Archibald, Don, 207
Arnold, Art, 7
Baada Point, 16
Bahokus Peak, 21
Baker, Dr., 204
Barker, Dorothy (Dankert), 92, 215
Beebe, Mary Ann, 195
Bernier, Betty (Pedersen), 27, 138, 180, 195, 196, 207
Big Bertha, 85
Bloedel Donovan, 113
Blomgren, Joe, 6, 114, 144, 212
Blomgren, Virginia, 6, 167, 186
Blomgren, Virginia (Huling), 29, 212
Blore, Bea, 170
Bombardier, Chet, 261
Boreson, Stan, 200
Bowlby, Bob, 10, 14, 33, 35, 221, 250
Bowlby, June, 144, 157, 237, 262
Brager Brothers Logging, 7
Burr, Dorothy, 73, 122, 227
Burr, Dorothy (Smith), 24, 137, 153, 163, 225
Burr, Ed, 207
Burr, Ivan, 163
Burr, Ray, 7
Burton, Vern, 215
Camp Hayden, 49, 50, 51
Cape Flattery, 22, 242, 250

Capos, Pete, 184, 207, 261
Cays, Glen, 206
Cays, Toots (Feight), 206
Claplanhoo, Ed, 249
Clark, Claude, 210
Clark, Steve, 17
Clemons, Don, 178
Cline, Dorothy, 130
Cline, Wayne, 190
Coast Trader, 241
Cochehour, Dwight, 86
Cone, Charles Edward, 35
Consford, Grover, 86
Cowan, John, 26
Cowan, Marge, 78, 194, 196, 208
Cowan-Jenson, Marge (McDonald), 26
Crippen, Jim, 7
Crippen, Wally, 5
Crown Zellerbach, 18, 21, 121, 122, 184
Deinis, Marge, 9, 18, 50, 123, 152, 193, 199
Dey, Lewis, 20, 237
Dickinson, Virginia, 205
Dirty Dora, 85
Duncan, Ed, 19, 87, 210, 211, 215, 260, 263, 267
Duncan, May, 205
Dungeness School, 19
Dunlap, Betty (Ryser), 9, 19, 131
Dunlap, Delbert "Nig", 184
Dunlap, Delbert (Nig), 10
Dunlap-Archibald, Vay (McHone), 10, 26, 124, 134, 153, 205
Early, Cecil, 243
Early, George, 91, 101, 243, 263
Eberle, Betty, 205

Here On the Home Front

Echternkamp, Henry, 10, 154, 271

Eckenberg, Fred, 43

Ediz Hook, 18, 45, 105, 200

Edmundston, 241

Elvrum, Bub, 125, 201

Elvrum, Darrel (Bub), 20, 133

Ferguson, Van, 207

Fernandez, Albert, 212

Flanders, Ross, 241

Fleck, William "Rod", 5

Fletcher, Bert, vii, 11, 88, 90, 101, 103, 109, 114, 158, 213, 228, 240, 259

Fletcher, Elizabeth (Huelsdonk), 23, 244

Fletcher, Estene, 91

Fletcher, Frank, 211

Fletcher, Fred, 29

Fletcher, Henry, 88

Fletcher, John, 23, 244

Fletcher, Lena, 29

Fletcher, Walt, 271

Fort Camosun, 242

Foster, Gene, 10

Freshwater Bay, 23

Frost, Jack, 113, 115

Fuhrman, Adria (Kaemmle), 220

Fuhrman, Walt, 33, 79, 89, 175, 196, 211

Gaydeski, Lawrence, 5, 17, 81, 125, 135, 152, 157, 170, 173, 219, 227, 240, 259, 263

Gaydeski, Steven, 17

Goodwin, Pa, 256

Gorham, Lee, 203

Gossage, Noss, 190

Green, Harvey, vii, 67, 70, 97, 147, 152, 242, 262

Hagadorn, Harry, 89, 90

Halverson, Inez, 24

Halverson, Inez (Halvi), 134

Hayden, Brigadier General John L., 49

Heathers, Rita, 195

Holenstein, W. M., 95

Holman, Bud, 183

Holman, Viola, 134, 205

Huggins, Del, 232

Huggins, Muriel, 235

Jardeen, Bill, 190

Jarvis, John, 11, 37, 47, 144, 158, 178, 213, 225, 239

Jones, Alton, 143

Jones, Eunice, 142, 210

Kalaloch, 5, 14, 16, 17, 65, 83, 123

Keller, Lillian (Lander), 152

Kelm, Arthur, 136, 190

Kelm, Jackie, 113

Kerschner, Bill, 89

Kettle, Toni (Becker), 19, 194

Kitchel, Lloyd, 190

Klahn, Darrell, 79, 97, 173, 189, 235, 244, 267

Klahn, Jim, 78

Klepps, Winnie, 195

Konopaski, Raleigh, 78

Kritter, Bill, 208

La Push, 15, 16, 26, 29, 35, 62, 65, 67, 73, 77, 81, 83, 88, 109, 140, 168, 186, 204, 209, 231, 249

Lake Crescent, 7, 152, 153

Lane, Glen, 47

Lane, Leo, 48

Laramie, Cye, 47

Leppell, Edna (Gentry), 199

Leppell, John, 6, 23, 79, 80, 82, 85, 109, 119, 131, 173, 189, 196, 201, 224, 243

Lucken, Maynard, 79, 125, 135, 175, 183, 195, 202

Lucken, Pearl, 135, 152, 184, 202, 260

Maneval, Ed, 7

Manning, Elsie Mae (Gilbert), 36

Mansfield, Jim, 41, 179, 197

Mansfield, Pat, 153

Mansfield, Pat (Blevins), 11, 41, 80

Mansfield, Tom, 175

WWII In Clallam County

Masonic Temple, 19, 200
Maupin, Eddy, 93
Maxfield, Art, 86
Maxfield, Frances, 86, 138, 176, 195, 249
McDonald, Wally, 208
McGuire, George, 34
McHone, Larry, 8, 123, 145
McInnes, Doug, vii, 19, 20, 39, 154, 156, 215
McNally, Jim, 186
Merchant, Mickey, 243
Micheau, Dave, 260
MIcheau, Jackie, 260
MITCHELL MONUMENT, 117
Mitchell, Elsie (Winters), 117
Mitchell, Pastor Archie, 117
Moose Hall, 19
Murray, Bart, 186
Nelson, John, 9, 14, 19, 50, 131, 193, 199, 201
Nelson, June, 9, 13, 18, 152, 193, 200
Nelson, Marlyn, 10, 154, 271
Noblette, William, 97
Olson, Jack, 47, 80, 88, 143, 177, 185, 211
Olympic Theater, 153, 199, 201, 202, 203, 204, 208, 212, 213, 227
Owl Mountain, 155
Ozette, 15, 16, 26, 33, 55, 56, 57, 58, 59, 60, 62, 63, 186, 189, 221, 250, 251
Palmer, Betty, 204
Palmer, Chuck, 156, 204
Palmer, Larry, 156
Palmer, Phil, 156
Paul, Ella, 134, 135
Paul, Warren, 26, 204
Paulson, Eldon, 261
Pederson, Elmer, 30
Peninsula Plywood, 184
Port Angeles Western Railroad, 186, 190

Porter, Beverly, 49, 127, 145, 164, 170, 179, 186, 197, 247
Price, Glen, 29, 176, 184, 207, 208
Price, Ivy, 207
Price, Ken, 207
Pyramid Peak, 152
Quillayute Union High School, 87, 215, 265
Rayonier, 136, 138, 144, 184, 193, 262
Richards, Gordon, 50
Robinson, June, 214
Ruby Beach, 13, 14, 17, 18, 23, 25, 109, 126, 167, 177, 244, 245, 251
Ruel and Vedder, 197
Rupp, Boyd, 14, 119, 242, 249
Sappho Camp, 113
Sarnowoski, Howard, 180
Schlaeter, Boyd, 25
Selfridge, Kirk, 243
Sequim High School, 19, 20, 36, 39, 131
Shaw, Fred, 82, 97, 195, 204
Shearer, Ron, vii, 10, 13, 24, 29, 79, 86, 110, 126, 140, 163, 167, 196, 219, 225, 227, 231, 249
Shi-Shi, 21
Shrader, Grahame F., 253
Signal Corp, 24, 30
Simmons, Jackie (Kelm), 136, 194
Simmons, Myron, 26, 82, 113, 189, 204, 205
Sinnema, Daisy (Smith), 93
Slather, Will, 204
Smith, Dave, 210
Smith, Duncan, 7
Smith, Leroy, 225
Spath, Myron, 215
Spoelstra, Ted, 7
Stovall, Norman, 247
Strait of Juan De Fuca, 37, 123
Streeter, Blonde, 208

Here On the Home Front

Streeter, Duke, 210
Streeter, Jean, 195
Sylvia, Donna, 194
Tatoosh Island, 241
Taylor, Doreen, 247
Taylor, Jess, 262
Thornton, Eleanor, 200
Tuffy and Taffy, 105
USO, 18, 167, 193
Van, Vic, 238
Vedder, Russell, 95
Virginia I, 241

Waadah Island, 21, 22, 249
Wahlgren, Lloyd, 204
Watson, Merle, 47, 184
Webber, Bert, 253
Wentworth, Bill, 177
Wittenborn, Arthur, 271
Wittenborn, Ernie, 210
Wittenborn, Joelene, 185, 195, 203, 210, 257
Wittenborn, Joelene (Goodie), 87, 211
Wood, George, 18, 121, 130, 219
Zinter, Ruth (Dankert), 92, 215

Made in the USA
San Bernardino, CA
11 February 2015